# UNDERSTANDING KARBALA

ABRIDGED & ADAPTED FROM THE
ORIGINAL WORK OF

**THE GRAND AYATOLLAH SAYYID
MUHAMMAD SAEED AL-HAKEEM**

MOHAMED ALI
ALBODAIRI

THE MAINSTAY
FOUNDATION

Author: Mohamed Ali Albodairi

Published by: The Mainstay Foundation

© 2017 The Mainstay Foundation

Printed in the United States.

ISBN: 978-1943393091

To the men of vision, foresight, and judgment whose sacrifices
preserved the faith of our Grand Prophet Muhammad

# CONTENTS

# AUTHOR'S PREFACE

In August 2015, the Mainstay Foundation organized and facilitated an educational retreat in the Holy City of Najaf. Imam Ali ibn Abu Talib, the cousin and son-in-law of the Prophet and the first of the Immaculate Imams, is buried at the heart of the old city. It is also home to one of the oldest and most respected seminaries of the Muslim world. For centuries Najaf has been a center of learning and guidance for Muslims worldwide. Our retreat in Najaf was organized for twenty young professionals from the United States, the United Kingdom, and Canada. Through the 10-day retreat, the group was able to connect, engage, and benefit from the scholars of the *hawza* (Islamic seminary) as well as the numerous cultural and educational institutions in the old city. They attended lectures and seminars by prominent seminary professors, visited the schools and dormitories of seminary students, and had engaging discussions with the scholars. These sessions were mutually beneficial as ideas were freely shared and discussed between the scholars and their guests.

The western professionals deepened their understanding of the seminary's rich heritage, while the scholars expressed appreciation for the professionals' openness and outlook on community affairs and their relationship with the seminary. The group also had a first-hand look at the old libraries carrying the tremendous wealth of knowledge that the seminary continues to safeguard and uphold. This is in addition to the obvious blessing of spending early mornings and late nights at the shrine of the Commander of the Faithful Imam Ali. At every moment, the group was either intellectually engaged or spiritually charged and uplifted – something unique to the city that hosts the sacred shrine of the Commander of the Faithful.

During our stay in the Holy City of Najaf, we had the distinct honor and privilege of visiting Grand Ayatollah Al-Hakeem. His office and home is an unassuming one-story building featuring clean white walls, bookcases filled with literature, and simple couches for visiting guests. As the group walked in, His Eminence and his sons greeted us with their pleasant smiles and welcoming arms. And as we sat down on the couches in the modestly furnished room, the Grand Ayatollah welcomed us enthusiastically despite his old age. He sat down at the same level as all of us, on the same mandarin-colored furniture. It was humbling to see the humility of such an individual.

We asked His Eminence to bless us with some words of wisdom. He spoke calmly but with a passion. During his short talk he emphasized the great potential of the Shia Muslim community. He said there were four factors to our strength: the legacy of Imam Hussain, the process of *ijtihad*, the Awaited Imam Mahdi, and selfless individuals who serve a higher purpose. "Don't say we don't have influence, power, and support. We do have power; a great deal of it. Do not be overwhelmed by groups with special interests. We act with what we have. We have our creed. We can do much. We simply must understand and utilize the great heritage left to us by our immaculate leaders."

His Eminence also stressed on three priorities for the Shia: creed, passion, and good morals. He spoke of the importance of our creed and how it must be cared for and protected. In addition, he stressed the significance of embracing our passion and not neglecting the emotional dimension of our being, especially in connection to our creed and what we hold sacred. Finally, the Grand Ayatollah told the group that it is of utmost importance to just simply be good people. He advised those present to be sincere, faithful, and pious. He stressed heavily on sincerity, and you could see the candor in his demeanor.

The session ended with the group's earnest show of appreciation for the Grand Ayatollah's time. As the majority of the group exited, I stayed sitting with His Eminence along with a few of my colleagues. By the time of our visit to Najaf, we had been working for several months on researching, studying, understanding, and translating some of the works of the Grand Ayatollah.

As I was the person responsible for putting this book together, I had a few questions to follow up with the Grand Ayatollah and following up on some of our previous conversations. Two of my colleagues asked poignant questions regarding the nuances and subtleties of the Grand Ayatollah's work, and I benefitted greatly from their insight. Finally, Abathar Tajaldeen and Jalal Moughania, who helped me immensely in researching and writing this book, followed up on the conversation with specific questions about the major concepts and conclusions of the Grand Ayatollah's works.

In order to realize the gravity of undertaking such work, one would have to understand the weight of the likes of Grand Ayatollah Al-Hakeem. Not only is he one of the leading jurists of his time, he comes from a rich heritage of scholarship and leadership. He is the grandson of Grand Ayatollah Muhsen Al-Hakeem who was the undisputed leading jurist of his time, known as *Marja' Al-Ta'ifa*.

Having survived the torture of eight years of imprisonment under the Baathist regime, and the execution of over sixty family members, Grand Ayatollah Al-Hakeem refused to leave the country. He would insist that if the scholars did not remain in Najaf, the heritage of the great seminary would be lost. Thus, he would be at the vanguard of protecting the seminary against all the challenges and obstacles it would face.

We huddled on the ground around the Grand Ayatollah – a sight I will never forget – and listened closely to his words. Being in his presence was no ordinary affair. His humbleness was awe-inspiring, his passion was captivating, and his sincerity was truly comforting. What was even more humbling was seeing his appreciation for our questions and inquiries. We delved into another discussion with the Grand Ayatollah focusing on one of his great works *Faji'at Al-Taff* – the Tragedy of Karbala – addressing some of the most fundamental cornerstones of our faith and heritage.

Why did Imam Hussain sacrifice as he did? What was the context in which this sacrifice and tragedy took place? What was the role of the remainder of the Household of the

Prophet before and after the tragedy? What was Imam Hussain's goal and how did he triumph despite the grand massacre?

He answered every one of our questions with a sincere passion. He laid out a framework through which we can understand the mission, sacrifices, and triumphs of our Imams. We went back and forth on different aspects of his work and the intention and purpose he had in writing as he did. The discussion carried on for quite some time and gave us greater depth into a process we had already begun – translating this great work.

Several months prior to meeting with the Grand Ayatollah in August 2015, the idea was born to write an English book based on his original work. In a previous meeting, the Grand Ayatollah had inspired us to translate *Faji'at Al-Taff* in a way that would be understandable to the English reader. He said, "Show the tragedy to the world. Show them the purpose of our mourning and commemorations. Show them the essence behind Imam Hussain's sacrifice."

Therefore, this book is by no means a direct translation of the original work. The original is a massive encyclopedia of referenced arguments, detailed examples, and insightful analysis. This book, *Understanding Karbala*, is an abridged version of the original work that was adapted for an English reading audience.

The purpose of this book is to highlight some of the priorities that the Grand Ayatollah laid out, and be inspired by the strength that lies within us. We wish to show the reader the gravity and necessity of Imam Hussain's tragic sacrifice.

We wish to shed light on the role our Imams played in preserving the faith.

Above all, we wish to study the movement of our Imams and derive a theoretical framework that we can base our lives upon. We wish to learn from their sacrifices and triumphs.

We pray that we were able to achieve this goal.

First, we must admit the great difficulty that comes with attempting to translate the Holy Quran. Muslim scholars have pondered on the meanings of the holy text for centuries, and our understanding of its verses only grows deeper as time passes. The process of translation always begs us to find precise meanings for the passages that we translate. But when we encounter the majesty of the Holy Quran, we find ourselves incapable of understanding, let alone translating, its true and deep meanings. We turned to the works of translators who have attempted to do this before. Although no translation can do justice to the Holy Quran, we found that the translation of Ali Quli Qarai to be the most proper in understanding when compared to the understanding of the text as derived by our grand scholars. As such, we decided to rely on Qarai's translations throughout this book, with some adaptations that allowed us to weave the verses more properly with the rest of the work.

A second great limitation came with translation of the narrations of the Grand Prophet Muhammad and his Holy Household. Their words are ever so deep and ever so powerful. We attempted to convey these passages to the reader in a tone that is understandable without deviating from the essence of the words of these immaculate personalities. We pray that we were successful in this endeavor.

Finally, we would like to acknowledge the individuals without whom this work would not have been possible. First, we must thank Grand Ayatollah Al-Hakeem, who inspired us to embark on the project. We must also thank Sayyid Riyadh Al-Hakeem and Sayyid Muhammad Hussain Al-Hakeem, who were instrumental during the process of writing and publishing this book.

Most importantly, we thank the Almighty for granting us such a unique opportunity and allowing us the tremendous honor to be able to partake in this project.

*Mohamed Ali Albodairi*

# ABOUT THE GRAND AYATOLLAH

His Eminence Grand Ayatollah Muhammad Saeed Al-Hakeem was born in the Holy City of Najaf in 1934. His father, Ayatollah Muhammad Ali Al-Hakeem, was a prominent scholar of his time. He grew under the tutelage of his father who began to teach him the basic courses of Islamic sciences before the age of ten.

Since his youth, His Eminence was known for his knowledge, ethics, and piety. He was respected amongst his peers and teachers for his keen understanding of the religious sciences and critical approach in discussion. He was always alongside his father in the gatherings of scholarly learning and intellectual discourse.

Grand Ayatollah Muhammad Saeed Al-Hakeem was given special attention by his maternal grandfather Grand Ayatollah Muhsen Al-Hakeem, who assigned his grandson the task of reviewing the manuscripts of his well renowned jurisprudential encyclopedia *Mustamsak Al-ʿUrwa Al-Wuthqa*. In the course of reviewing the manuscripts, His Eminence would discuss the text with his grandfather. Through those sessions he gained a great wealth of knowledge and showcased his understanding and skill in the Islamic sciences.

During his time at the Islamic Seminary of Najaf, His Eminence studied under some of the most prominent scholars. Those scholars included his father, his maternal grandfather, Grand Ayatollah Hussain Al-Hilli, and Grand Ayatollah Abulqasim Al-Khoei.

At the age of thirty-four, after having spent more than two decades of his life in the pursuit of religious learning, he began offering *bahth kharij* (advanced seminars) in the principles of jurisprudence. Two years later, he began offering advanced seminars in jurisprudence based on the books of Al-Shaykh Al-A'dham Murtadha Al-Ansari and his grandfather Grand Ayatollah Muhsen Al-Hakeem. Since then, His Eminence would continue to teach advanced seminars despite the challenges and obstacles he would face.

Along with his teachers and peers, His Eminence was active in public affairs ever since he joined the seminary. He was amongst the group of scholars that supported Grand Ayatollah Muhsen Al-Hakeem in his movement against Communist influence in Iraq. In 1963, Grand Ayatollah Muhammad Saeed Al-Hakeem signed the notable petition from the seminary that denounced President Abdul Salam Arif's attempt to impose Communism in Iraq.

When the Baathist regime overthrew its predecessor and took control of Iraq, His Eminence continued his activism against the state's dictatorial policies. Most notably, he would defy Baathist threats to execute anyone who would fulfill the ritual of walking toward the city of Karbala as a commemoration of the sacrifices made there fourteen centuries ago. Because of this defiance, the Grand Ayatollah became a pursued target of the Baathist regime and was forced into hiding until the regime finally closed the case. Yet despite all the harassment and persecution, His Eminence would remain in Najaf and refuse to join the exodus away from Baathist tyranny. He saw the exodus as a threat to the existence of Najaf's seminary, and so decided to stay in the city to ensure its continuity.

On May 9th, 1983, after the Hakeem family's refusal to support the Baathist regime during the Iran-Iraq war, many of the family's members were arrested, including the Grand Ayatollah himself. There, they faced constant interrogation and all kinds of torture. They were beaten with nightsticks and subjected to electric shocks, to name a couple of the most used torture methods. Diseases began to spread, with no access to any medical assistance. Still, the family's fortitude was not broken and they persevered.

Shortly after the mass imprisonment of the family, the Grand Ayatollah began offering classes in Quranic exegesis. He found no other books or sources for study in the Baathist prison system other than an old and worn copy of the Holy Quran. The wardens soon found out about this course and forced him to stop teaching. Nonetheless, religious discussions and commemorations continued in secrecy throughout their years of imprisonment. During those years, a total of sixteen members of the Hakeem family were executed by the regime.

In 1985, the remainder of the imprisoned members of the Hakeem family was moved to Abu Ghraib prison, which was a lower security prison at the time. There, the Grand Ayatollah found an opportunity to continue teaching the advanced seminars he had offered before imprisonment.

Since most of the inmates with him were highly educated seminarians and students of his, he quickly seized the opportunity.

Finally, on June 7, 1991, His Eminence and the remainder of the Hakeem family were released from prison. That, however, did not mean an end to Baathist harassment. Baathist authorities badgered him in an attempt to name him an official state designated religious authority. He definitively refused such offers, asserting that religious authority is and must always be independent. Because of his firm position, the state imposed a great deal of restrictions on the Grand Ayatollah. Amongst those restraints included a ban on publishing any of his books and scholarly work and broad restrictions on his travel.

After the passing of Grand Ayatollah Abulqasim Al-Khoei the following year, many scholars and seminarians petitioned His Eminence to assume the obligations and duties of Marja' – the religious authority to whom the believers refer to in issues of law. In compliance with the incessant petitions of students and peers, he put forward his views on Islamic law and practice and became one of the most prominent religious authorities of the time. He continued his scholarly work, writing and teaching across the fields of Islamic sciences. Currently based in the Holy City of Najaf, Grand Ayatollah Al-Hakeem is one of the leading contemporary religious authorities for Shia Muslims worldwide.

# INTRODUCTION

*In the Name of God, the Most Beneficent, the Most Merciful*

There are two major theories debated by historians in regards to the tragedy of Karbala. A group of historians believe that the events were the natural conclusion of human choices. They see Imam Hussain's actions and decisions as bound by the limitations of natural human tendencies and outlook.

The other group of historians believes that the events of Karbala were the culmination of a divinely orchestrated plan. That what happened in Karbala was not the conclusion of Imam Hussain's human tendencies, but of a higher will that saw the tragedy as a necessary component of that divine plan.

## A HUMAN PLAN

Those who believe that the tragedy at Karbala was the culmination of a human plan claim that Imam Hussain had orchestrated a revolt driven by personal motivations; that the tragedy that transpired in Karbala was a natural consequence of those ambitions.

They hold that Imam Hussain's methods in dealing with the circumstances of his time and his opponents – Yazid[1] specifically – were the main cause of the events of Karbala. They reject any notion that divine will or inspiration played a role in Imam Hussain's choices and journey.

Some even allege that Imam Hussain's ambitions had led him to lose his better judgment and miscalculate his course of action. They speculate that he may have been misled by the Kufans' false promises, or beguiled by ibn Al-Zubayr's[2] feigned advice.

This strand of analysis has led these historians to believe that Imam Hussain was killed in a struggle for power – that he was killed by his own ambition. They assert that he miscalculated his power, naively underestimated his enemies, and fell into the trap of the deceptive Kufans. They claim that even though some in Medina had the foresight to see the consequences of his campaign, and advised him against it, he unwisely ignored their counsel.

Such conclusory judgments have been adopted by a significant group of Muslims[3] who do not ascribe to the Shia school of thought.[4]

---

[1] Yazid ibn Muawiya ibn Abu Sufyan, the second ruler of the Umayyad Dynasty. His reign lasted only for three years, beginning in 680 CE. The tragedy of Karbala took place in that same year. –Eds.

[2] Abdullah ibn Al-Zubayr, the son of a famed companion of the Prophet. Abdullah led a revolt against the Umayyad Dynasty a few years after the events of Karbala. –Eds.

[3] See, for example: Ibn Asakir, *Tareekh Dimashq*, 14:239.

[4] Commonly known as Shia Muslims. –Eds.

# A DIVINE PLAN

The second theory explains the events of Karbala as a culmination of a divinely drawn and guided plan. The supporters of this theory say that God had given Imam Hussain a covenant – delivered through his grandfather the Prophet – and drawn for him a plan that built up to the tragedy of Ashura. That tragedy and Imam Hussain's undying sacrifice would save Islam from the brink of compromise it had reached. Imam Hussain would become the nation's light of guidance and its ship of salvation – one that would be forever imprinted in the hearts and minds of Muslims by God's will.[5]

Imam Hussain was divinely chosen for his unmatched personality, noble virtues, and stellar character. He took the lead role in implementing the divine plan after the passing of the Prophet, his father Imam Ali, and brother Imam

---

[5] The Grand Ayatollah argues that Imam Hussain was divinely chosen to implement a plan drawn by God Almighty to save the Muslim nation from misguidance and bring it back to the teachings of the Holy Quran and the Prophet Muhammad. This should not be misconstrued to mean that the Battle of Karbala and its tragic events were *predestined*. Rather, all sides in this struggle had their free will in choosing whether to side with tyranny or righteousness. The 'divine plan' is a reference to the commands given to Imam Hussain by his grandfather the Prophet, which were given to the Prophet by God Almighty. Imam Hussain chose out of his own volition to follow these divine commands when he left Medina towards Mecca, and ultimately towards Kufa. The divine plan had anticipated the choices of Yazid and his army – choices which were the product of their free will and their base desires. Even on the day of the battle, each soldier in either camp continued to have the freedom of choice between siding with Imam Hussain or his enemies. On that day, there were some – like Al-Hurr ibn Yazid Al-Riyahi – who exercised this freedom and abandoned the army of Yazid to fight alongside Imam Hussain. –Eds.

Hassan. Some of the divine wisdoms in this regard are revealed to us, and some are not.

In the end, Imam Hussain manifested God's will and was successful in realizing the divine plan. He achieved what he set out to attain and crowned his movement with an astounding victory. His victory was not in battle – that wasn't his aspiration. Imam Hussain's victory was saving the faith and bringing quintessential reform in the nation of his grandfather, the Holy Prophet.

Thus, those who had advised him to refrain from making the journey towards Kufa had simply been oblivious to the wisdom behind God's plan. The same had been true years ago when the Prophet entered into the Treaty of Hudaybiya,[6] though his companions disliked its terms. Imam Hassan faced a similar situation when his companions berated him for his treaty with Muawiya.[7] But as the Commander of the Faithful once said, "People are enemies of what they do not know."[8] They are ignorant of the wisdom behind these things, and so – wittingly or not – they become opponents of God's divine plan.

---

[6] The Treaty of Hudaybiya was a treaty entered into between Prophet Muhammad and the Meccan tribe of Quraysh in the year 6 AH. The Prophet was chided by his followers, as they did not like the terms of the treaty. However, God revealed the following verse in commemoration of this occasion, "Indeed We have inaugurated for you a clear victory" (The Holy Quran, 48:1). Though the peace did not last for the stipulated ten years, historians believe that the treaty was crucial to the continued existence of Islam in these formative years. –Eds.

[7] Muawiya ibn Abu Sufyan, the first ruler of the Umayyad Dynasty. – Eds.

[8] Al-Radi, *Nahj al-Balagha*, Hadith 438.

*Textual Support for the Divine Plan Theory*

We, as Shia Muslims, adopt this second theory in regards to Imam Hussain's actions. This is because we believe in the immaculate nature of our Imams – they are divinely appointed and guided leaders that are tasked with protecting the Message after the Prophet. Thus, as an effect of God's justice and mercy His appointees do not err or misguide. They are immaculate. This immaculateness is characteristic of the Prophet, first and foremost, Lady Fatima, and the Twelve Holy Imams.

The logical necessity of immaculateness and divine guidance of those delivering and protecting the Message naturally flows from our doctrinal principle of divine justice. This principle alone should suffice in proving the point above. Nevertheless, our books are flooded with textual evidence that support this argument. We will provide further context and support by mentioning a few of these texts here.

It is narrated that Imam Baqir was once asked why his forefathers – Imam Imam Ali, Imam Hassan, and Imam Hussain – led battles that ended in military defeat. The Imam replied,

> *God the Almighty had destined that for them. He had declared it and made it a certain reality… It was through prior knowledge given to them by the Messenger of God that they, Ali, Hassan and Hussain, rose [for battle]. And it is by such knowledge that whoever remained silent amongst us, was as such.*[9]

In another narration, Imam al-Sadiq says,

---

[9] Al-Kulayni, *Al-Kafi*, 1:262.

*God the Almighty revealed a book to His Prophet before his death. He told him, 'Oh Muhammad, this is your will to the selected amongst your family members...' So the Prophet gave it to the Commander of the Faithful and commanded him to open the first seal and to follow the instructions within. The Commander of the Faithful [did so], then gave it to his son al-Hassan [with the same instructions. Imam Hassan opened the second seal] and followed the instructions within. He then gave it to Imam Hussain, who opened the next seal. He found written within, 'Set out with a group to your martyrdom, for they will not be martyred except by your side. Sell yourself for [the pleasure of] God the Almighty.' And so he did. He gave the book to Imam Ali ibn al-Hussain [before his martyrdom....*[10]

In another narration relating back to the Prophet, we are told that the Messenger of God once delivered a sermon in which he told the people of the massacre and martyrdom of his grandson Imam Hussain. When the people began to cry and wail, the Prophet exclaimed, "Would you cry, though you would not support him?"[11]

In another narration, the Prophet told a group of his companions, "Gabriel has told me that my son will be killed in the land of Taf.[12] He brought me these sands [from that land] and told me that he would be buried there."[13]

The Imams did not stop at a general foretelling of Imam Hussain's martyrdom. They mentioned details such as the

---

[10] Al-Kulayni, *Al-Kafi*, 1:280.

[11] Al-Khawarizmi, *Maqtal Al-Hussain*, 1:164.

[12] Taf is another name given to the land of Karbala. –Eds.

[13] Al-Tabarani, *Al-Mu'jam Al-Kabir*, 3:107.

location of the massacre, the timing, and other details about the event. And not only did they foretell of the battle of Karbala, they also encouraged their followers to join Imam Hussain on his journey.

The Prophet told his companions, "This son of mine [i.e. Hussain] will be killed in a land called Karbala. Whoever lives to see that day should endeavor to be his supporter."[14]

*Imam Hussain Foretells his Martyrdom*

Imam Hussain himself would speak of these details throughout his life and during his journey toward Karbala. He mentioned some details in his sermon in Mecca just as he was heading towards Karbala.

Imam Ali Zayn Al-Abideen narrates that when he was with his father on his journey toward Karbala

> *He would not set camp in any location or move through it except that he would mention the story of John the Baptist and how he was martyred. One day he said, 'Did you not know that the world is so worthless in the eyes of God such that the head of John the Baptist was presented to a harlot of the Israelites?'[15]*

---

[14] Ibn Asakir, *Tareekh Dimashq*, 14:224.

[15] Al-Mufid, *Al-Irshad*, 2:132. For an account of John the Baptist's martyrdom, see: Arastu, *God's Emissaries*, 591-92. The New Testament contains a similar account. See: Mark 14:1-12. The reader should not confuse the expression "the world is so worthless in the eyes of God" with indifference or lethargy towards such a great tragedy. Muslims believe that God, the Wise and Beneficent, would not create anything that is worthless. However, relative to the life of the hereafter, this worldly life is indeed worthless. Thus, the greatest tragedies befell the most esteemed of religious figures, not because they were forsaken by their Lord, but because their perseverance in this world was their avenue towards God's pleasure. It is through this perseverance that they gained

Imam Hussain would also speak to Omar ibn Saad and assured him that what was foretold – that Omar ibn Saad would kill Imam Hussain – was sure to happen. He also assured him of the remainder of the prophecy; that Omar would not live long after his crimes but for a few days.

Imam Hussain would tell Omar to his face,

> *Oh Omar! You will kill me thinking that the imposter the son of an imposter [i.e. Yazid ibn Muawiya] would appoint you to the government of Rey and Gorgan![16] By God, you will never take pleasure in that! It is a promise that has been made. Do as you wish, as you will not find pleasure after my death in this world or the next. It is as if I can see your head hoisted on a cane over the city of Kufa, while children pelt it with stones....[17]*

Despite all this, Imam Hussain was adamant to head toward Kufa and Karbala. He did not heed the advice of those who told him to stay in Mecca, assuring him that he would be safe if he stayed near the sacred Great Mosque of Mecca.[18] But the Imam did not wish that the sanctity of the Grand

---

high regard in the eyes of God and the eyes of men. All these meanings are buried in the statement that Imam Hussain made and are conveyed in the Arabic text. Since they could not be embedded in a simple translation of the statement, we have deferred it to this footnote. –Eds.

[16] Rey and Gorgan were provinces of the Umayyad state. They are located in the northern part of modern day Iran. –Eds.

[17] Al-Khawarizmi, *Maqtal Al-Hussain*, 2:8.

[18] The Grand Mosque of Mecca, known in Arabic as *Al-Masjid Al-Haram* – literally, 'the sacred mosque' – is one of the holiest sites in Islam. It houses the *Kaaba*, a cubical structure built by the prophets Abraham and Ishmael as a site of worship. Muslims around the globe direct themselves toward the *Kaaba* in their prayers. The Grand Mosque of Mecca is also a destination for pilgrims from around the globe, especially during the annual *Hajj* season when millions descend upon the sacred mosque to perform the rites of the *Hajj*. –Eds.

Mosque be defiled if the Umayyad army shed his blood there. And when others advised him to head south to Yemen, he simply rebuked their advice and did not discuss their suggestions.

While on his journey, Imam Hussain met a poet by the name of Farazdaq and asked him about the people of Iraq. Farazdaq replied, "Their hearts are with you, but their swords are with the Umayyad clan. Judgment will come from the heavens. God will do what He wills." Imam Hussain replied,

> *True. But it is the will of God, and He does as He pleases. Every day our Lord is engaged in some work. If He were to dictate things that please us, we praise Him, thank Him, and ask His support in our thankfulness. And if His dictates are to stand in the way of our hopes, it would not affect anyone whose intention is righteous and who is pious at heart.*[19]

Abdullah ibn Abbas also narrates that he met Imam Hussain as he was heading toward Iraq. Ibn Abbas relays that he had advised the Imam not to journey toward Iraq. But Imam Hussain replied, "Do you not know that my death will be there? And that my companions will face their demise there?" When ibn Abbas asked Imam Hussain how he could be so sure of this, he replied that "It is by a secret confided to me and a knowledge granted to me."[20]

---

[19] Al-Tabari, *Tareekh Al-Tabari*, 4:290.
[20] Al-Tabari, *Dalael Al-Imama*, 181.

*Prepared for Death*

Imam Hussain was prepared to meet his death. He knew exactly when and where he would be massacred along with his family and companions. During his journey, he would constantly foretell of the betrayal that he would face.

He even prepared to meet Al-Hurr ibn Yazid Al-Riyahi.[21] One day at dusk, he told his family and companions to head to a nearby river and get more water than they usually would in anticipation of the encounter and the coming days of thirst in the desert of Karbala.

Hurr, leading a battalion of the Umayyad army, met Imam Hussain in the vicinity of Kufa. After negotiating with Hurr, Imam Hussain conceded to lead his family and companions in a direction neither towards Kufa nor back towards Medina. There were a number of ways he could have headed that would have been 'neither towards Kufa nor back towards Medina.' But Imam Hussain chose to head north toward the land of Karbala, where Umayyad control was stronger. He did not back off into a territory where he may be able to evade Hurr's battalion and delay the battle until he could gather more forces. Rather, he headed straight into enemy territory, giving no heed to Yazid or his army.

Even then, he received a number of offers to change his path and head towards nearby towns or mountains where he may be able to fortify his forces. But he refused.

---

[21] Al-Hurr ibn Yazid Al-Riyahi was a commander in the Umayyad army. He led the battalion that intercepted Imam Hussain on his way to Kufa and did not allow him to proceed towards the city or return back to Medina. Hurr was a commander in the Umayyad army until the day of the Battle of Karbala, when he repented and joined the ranks of Imam Hussain's companions. –Eds.

He continued on his path away from any safe haven until he reached a barren land. He peered onto the land and declared, "Here is where we will rest our mounts and set our camp. Here is where our blood will be shed...."[22] In another narration, he added, "This is what my grandfather the Messenger of God had told me of before."[23]

*Implementing the Divine Plan*

All this proves that Imam Hussain's stance was the culmination of a divine plan. Had it been otherwise, the Prophet would have commanded him not to set out on this journey. His father the Commander of the Faithful would have advised against it. But instead, they encouraged people to support him in his stance. And of what we know of Imam Hussain's character, we must be certain that he would not have gone against their advice. Rather, they had encouraged him to set out on his journey and make his stance. It is even narrated that the Prophet had told him, "You have a status [reserved for you] that you will not attain except through martyrdom."[24]

## TWO THOUGHTS

Two final thoughts before delving deeper into the topic:

First, after showing that Imam Hussain's stance was the culmination of a divine plan, there is no need to go into the details of the historical account. If God had drawn that plan, all details of it were purposely crafted through divine

---

[22] Al-Khawarizmi, *Maqtal Al-Hussain*, 2:8.
[23] Ibn Tawus, *Al-Luhuf*, 49.
[24] Al-Khawarizmi, *Maqtal Al-Hussain*, 1:170.

wisdom. And because of what we know of Imam Hussain's immaculate nature, we must submit that he had implemented that divine plan in all its details, as delivered to him by the Holy Prophet.

Secondly, this brief discussion has illustrated the greatness of Imam Hussain's character and his unmatched will, determination, resolve and forbearance. How selfless must one be to fulfill a plan that will only end in his death and the massacre of his family and companions? How faithful must one be to submit to such a fate in complete subservience simply because it is divinely ordained? How great was his resolve, how big was his heart, and how encompassing was his vision? The answer: beyond what we can imagine.

# THE DEPTH OF TRAGEDY

Over time, the majority of Muslims, with the exception of the Shia, came to believe that the caliphate was a political position that can be legitimately passed down through hereditary rule. Shia belief holds the caliphate in a different light. They believe that the political power vested in the caliphate after the Prophet is a right divinely granted to the Immaculate Imams from the household of the Prophet Muhammad.[1] The rest of the Muslims did not make such a qualification, but saw the establishment of dynasties and empires as politically legitimate.

Still, most Muslims did condemn the coronation of Yazid as caliph after his father Muawiya. They list a number of reasons for this.

---

[1] The Shia do not believe that this grant was due to a hereditary right, a common mischaracterization of Shia Islam's creed. They do assert that the household of the Prophet were the safeguards of the faith and its political leadership after the passing of the Prophet. But this did not entitle all of the Prophet's bloodline to the claim of divine right. Rather, the divinely granted right and responsibility of leadership was bestowed upon a select few of the Prophet's progeny because of their impeccable character and qualifications. –Eds.

Firstly, this was the first instance after the Prophet where the highest political power in the nation was passed down by hereditary privilege. It was Muawiya who broke with the tradition of the first four caliphs revered in Sunni Islam, and established the precedent of hereditary rule by setting his son to rule after him. It was this form of hereditary rule that early Muslims had hoped to avoid after the death of the Prophet.[2]

Secondly, the means by which Muawiya hoped to install his son as successor were detested by many. He had relied on terror tactics, bribery, fraud, deception, and blackmail. And although these tactics were not unfamiliar to the Muslims, Muawiya's aims were averse to the elite of Quraysh. They had turned a blind eye when others implemented similar tactics because the aims and outcomes were in their favor. But now the tables had turned and Muawiya was acting adversely to their interests.

Thirdly, the fact that Yazid was grossly unfit to rule stood out, especially with so many companions of the Prophet and righteous followers with social standing available to take on the role. Foremost amongst these individuals was Imam Hussain himself, who was not only the sole legitimate leader according to Shia Muslims, but also a widely loved and respected religious figure for all Muslims.

In addition, Imam Hussain's call for reform was not a political movement. He was not rebelling with an ambition to gain power. His words never reflected political motivations. Instead, he spoke as an advisor and counselor to the Muslim

---

[2] See, for example: Al-Mutazili, *Sharh Nahj al-Balagha*, 6:43.

nation. As he mentioned to his half-brother Muhammad ibn al-Hanafiyya,

> *I do not revolt due to discontent [with God's blessings], nor out of arrogance. I did not rise as a corruptor, nor as an oppressor. Rather, I wish to call for reform in the nation of my grandfather. I wish to call for what is good, and to forbid what is evil. Whoever accepts me because I carry the truth, then God is the refuge of the honest. As for whoever rejects this call, I will be patient until God judges between me and the rejecters with His justice. Surely, He is the best of judges.*[3]

## UMAYYAD CRIMES AT KARBALA

Imam Hussain did nothing that would make him deserving of death or punishment, let alone the horrid crimes that befell him and his family at Karbala. To put some perspective on this, let us mention a few of the crimes of that massacre.

The greatest crime of that massacre was the murder of Imam Hussain – a figure of high religious status, impeccable character, and the grandson of the Prophet Muhammad.

The crime was compounded with the massacre of anyone who stood by Imam Hussain on that day. This included his children, brothers, cousins, and nephews – all of whom were close family members of the Prophet. This also included the vanguard of society who stood in support of Imam Hussain. Some of these individuals were close companions of the Prophet. Some were designated reciters of the Holy Quran in their communities. They were all known

---

[3] Ibn A'tham, *Al-Futuh*, 5:34.

for their stellar character, religious insight, great piety, and manifest charity. They were the best representatives of Islam.

The massacre extended to reach innocent children, including one infant child of Imam Hussain. It also extended to reach women who did not participate in the battle. The ruthlessness of the Umayyad army, representing the caliphate of Yazid, was unsurpassed. All this shows the disgusting criminality of the Umayyad army and its regime.

Even before the massacre had begun, the Umayyad army had shown its depraved character. They refused Imam Hussain's camp access to water, leaving women and children to wither of thirst. They did this despite the fact that only a few days before Imam Hussain had shared his camp's own water with a battalion of the Umayyad army – the same battalion that prevented him from reaching Kufa and wished to take him and his family as prisoners.

The army continued to show its viciousness even after the massacre by its treatment of the corpses of Imam Hussain and his companions. They did not stop at decapitating all their victims, hoisting their heads on the tips of spears, and parading them around as they traveled from city to city. They continued to maim and mutilate the bodies of the dead. Imam Hussain's body was trampled by horses. The Umayyad army did not allow for the burial of the bodies until three days after the massacre.

This was in addition to taking the women from the family of the Prophet, including his granddaughters, as captives. During the battle, they had burned Imam Hussain's camp setting fire to the tents of the women and children. They deliberately struck fear into the hearts of the widows and orphans. They pillaged the camp and looted what they could. They then paraded their captives across the state, from Karbala, to Kufa, to Damascus.

They did not stop at this. They tried to defile Imam Hussain's name even after his murder using their pulpits of propaganda. They sought to justify the massacre and disparage Hussain and his companions, but to no avail.

## The Muslim Conscience

The weight of the tragedy was amplified by a number of factors. For one, Imam Hussain was the last grandson of the Prophet. Imam Hussain and his brother Imam Hassan were very close to the Prophet and he loved them dearly. Now, the head of the Prophet's beloved grandson is being paraded in their city centers.

The nation remembered the words of their Prophet and of their commander Imam Ali, both of whom had anticipated and foretold of this tragic event. They had shown great sorrow for what would be done to Imam Hussain and had mourned him years before the tragedy. The Muslims remembered their Prophet's admonition to stand by Imam Hussain during this period, but they had been heedless to his words.

In addition, the Umayyad clan – in the stupor of their victory – carelessly began to relish their victory against Imam Hussain and claiming vengeance for their ancestors whom the Prophet had defeated in battle.[4]

---

[4] See, for example: Sibt ibn Al-Jawzi, *Tathkirat Al-Khawas*, 261.

This is in addition to the supernatural occurrences that took place during the tragedy which both Shia and Sunni historians relayed in their books. For example, they relay that Hussain took some of his blood and the blood of his infant child and lobbed it toward the heavens, but not a drop of it fell back to the earth.[5]

## POPULAR REACTIONS

If we look back at history, we find that the people of the time had a great deal of reverence for Imam Hussain and the family of the Prophet. So what happened that led the people to slight their emotional connection with this family and lead such a massacre against their Prophet's closest kin and companions?

Looking closely at history, we find that the people of the time were deceived by Muawiya's vile tactics. He had used terror and bribery to lead a nation away from its most revered icons. And we see that once the tragedy had occurred, the veil was lifted. The nation realized the great crime that it had committed and woke up to Muawiya's treachery.

The ruling authorities had treated Imam Hussain as a mischievous rebel. They attempted to paint him as a blasphemous revolutionary who sought to divide the nation and cause a great sedition. Through this characterization, they sought to justify their massacre. They attempted to vilify Imam Hussain so they could justify their decapitation of

---

[5] See, for example: Al-Tabari, *Tareekh Al-Tabari*, 4:343; Al-Asfahani, *Maqatil Al-Talibiyyin*, 59; Ibn Asakir, *Tareekh Dimashq*, 14:223.

corpses, mutilation of bodies, and massacre and imprisonment of the Prophet's family.

With this, the Umayyad government had reached the apex of its vile and domineering regime. It struck down anyone who dared to utter a word of dissent. Even after the massacre at Karbala, the Umayyad government would go on to perpetrate another massacre in the city of Medina after its inhabitants disavowed allegiance to Yazid. Shortly after that massacre, the Umayyad army brutally put down the rebellion of Abdullah ibn Al-Zubayr, using catapults to set siege to the Mecca. In that encounter, the Umayyad army went so far as to hit the Grand Mosque with their catapults and destroy a part of the holiest mosque in Islam.

This should have been enough to quell the flames of rebellion throughout the nation. The Ummayad dynasty's response to these rebellions was so quick and heavy handed, that no one would think of dissenting against the iron fist of the regime. But nonetheless, we saw that the accumulation of these tragedies had done so much to move the nation that many could not sit quietly in their wake.

*Denunciation*

There were many individual denunciations to the massacre of Karbala. We will not go through these instances, as we see that the popular and social reaction was of much greater importance. Any historical record which may have recounted reactions throughout much of the Muslim nation has been lost. However, the accounts of what happened in Kufa and Medina specifically are exceptionally well preserved.

In Kufa – a city known for its love of the Alid[6] family – the people of the city welcomed the defeated victims of the Umayyad army with cries and wails. The anguish of the tragedy was visible throughout the city. The women of the city mourned the death of Imam Hussain by beating their chests and their heads.[7]

As for Medina – the home of the Prophet and his Progeny – the news was welcomed with similar anguish.[8] And when the remainder of the victims of Karbala returned to Medina, they were welcomed with wails and cries befitting the trage-dy. As Imam Hussain's families entered Medina, not a single soul stayed at home, but all came to welcome the caravan of tragedies.[9]

Even in the Levant – a province controlled by the Umayyad clan and that knew nothing but Umayyad propaganda – de-nunciation of the tragedy was evident enough to be record-ed in books of history. It began by a few viziers in Yazid's court.[10] Even amongst the public, there was mourning and outcries, albeit in secrecy and caution.[11]

God knows how the rest of the Muslim nation reacted to the tragedy. Historians did not transcribe the reactions of the remainder of the Muslim provinces. But we can only imagine that the reaction was similar or even more pro-

---

[6] Alid is a reference to the descendants of Imam Ali ibn Abu Talib. – Eds.

[7] See, for example: Ibn A'tham, *Al-Futuh*, 5:139.

[8] Al-Yaqubi, *Tareekh Al-Yaqubi*, 2:246.

[9] Al-Asfahani, *Al-Aghani*, 5:75.

[10] Ibn Al-Atheer, *Usud Al-Ghaba*, 5:381.

[11] Al-Khawarizmi, *Maqtal Al-Hussain*, 2:61.

nounced, given that these lands were farther away from the Umayyad center of power in the Levant.

In addition, Imam Hussain had been using the last years of Muawiya's reign to spread his message. During that time, he utilized the hajj season to host a large conference of religious scholars, including companions of the Prophet.

He gathered the most learned amongst the pilgrims and began to recite to them the virtues of the family of the Prophet. He recited all the verses of the Quran that commended the progeny of the Prophet and explained them to everyone present. He mentioned to them all the sayings of the Prophet that praised his father Imam Ali, his mother Lady Fatima, and his brother Imam Hassan. He mentioned those sayings of the Prophet that praised him and he reminded those present of his closeness to his grandfather.

In all this, he was supported by a large number of companions that would bear witness to the truth of what he said. Anyone who was not witness to these truths would say, "By God, I have now heard it from credible and trustworthy companions of the Prophet."[12]

The mourning family of Imam Hussain – which was left with no men but an ailing Imam Ali ibn Hussain – saw that the tragedy had left fertile ground in which they could sow the seeds of truth. They utilized the tragedy to beseech the peoples' hearts. Through this, they were able to show the nation the gravity of its crime. They were able to spread the message of Imam Hussain and his predecessors – Imam Hassan, Imam Ali, and the Prophet Muhammad.

---

[12] Al-Tabrasi, *Al-Ihtijaj*, 2:18-19.

They did this in Karbala before the massacre occurred.[13] They did so again in the squares of Kufa[14] and in the palace of its governor.[15] They went on to do the same in the Levant[16] and in the court of Yazid.[17]

The massacre of Karbala was not the only tragedy that the Muslims had to decry. Only shortly after the massacre at Karbala, Yazid's army perpetrated another massacre in Medina. Then there was the siege of Mecca and the destruction of part of the Grand Mosque. But the martyrdom of Imam Hussain and the tragedy of Karbala remained the greatest in the heart of the Muslims.

*Regret*

Regret was also a pronounced public sentiment after the tragedy. It was most evident in those that had actually participated in the battle against Imam Hussain. Take for example Omar ibn Saad – the general that led the Umayyad army in Karbala. He would be seen leaving the court of ibn Ziyad, the governor of Kufa, saying, "No one has come with such a grave crime as me. I obeyed a miscreant like ibn Ziyad. I disobeyed my Just Lord. I severed a noble bond [with the Prophet]."[18] People began to disassociate from

---

[13] Ibn Shahrashoob, *Manaqib Aal Abu Talib*, 3:260.

[14] Ibn Tawuus, *Al-Luhuf*, 91-92.

[15] Al-Tabari, *Tareekh Al-Tabari*, 4:349-50.

[16] Al-Aalusi, *Rooh Al-Ma'ani*, 25:31.

[17] Ibn Tawuus, *Al-Luhuf*, 101.

[18] Sibt ibn Al-Jawzi, *Tathkirat Al-Khawas*, 259. Although Omar ibn Saad showed some signs of regret, it does not seem from the historical accounts that he had sincerely repented. He said these specific words while walking out of ibn Ziyad's court, having been rejected after asking for the prize he was promised. Thus, he showed this 'regret' only when his expectation for worldly rewards were not met. –Eds.

him and curse him whenever he would pass by. He was thus forced to sit in his home until he was killed.

Many people that did not participate in the battle also felt the sting of regret. Most of these individuals were not able to join Imam Hussain because they were imprisoned or otherwise prevented by ibn Ziyad, the governor of Kufa. Still, they felt the need to 'repent' for not having supported Imam Hussain in his cause and rose in rebellion after the massacre. Their movement was dubbed the Repenters' Revolt – *Thawrat Al-Tawwabeen.*

### Politicization

Lastly, there were factions that tried to politicize Imam Hussain's martyrdom and use it for their own political advantage. For example, Abdullah ibn Al-Zubayr – who was known for his hatred of Imam Hussain and the Alid family – would attempt to use Imam Hussain's name for this purpose. He would constantly disparage the people of Iraq and the people of Kufa specifically. But when he mentions Imam Hussain, he would say,

> *But he chose an honorable death over a wretched life. May God have mercy on Hussain's soul and dishonor his murderers. Can we trust these people after what they did to Hussain? Can we believe their word? Can we trust their promises?*[19]

Thus, he used Imam Hussain's martyrdom as a propaganda tool against his political rivals – namely the Umayyad authorities in Damascus.

---

[19] Al-Tabari, *Tareekh Al-Tabari,* 4:364.

## THE UMAYYAD STANCE

It is only natural that Yazid would have had a hand in the murder of Imam Hussain in Karbala. No one could deny that he must have been informed of ibn Ziyad's course of action and approved of it, let alone ordered it. Ibn Ziyad would not dare commit such an atrocity without the caliph's directive. Furthermore, ibn Ziyad had already killed Imam Hussain's messenger to Kufa, Muslim ibn Aqeel, and other supporters, such as Hani ibn Urwa, and sent their heads to Yazid.[20] If Yazid did not approve of ibn Ziyad's actions, as some claim, then he would have averted the tragedy as he had ample evidence that ibn Ziyad was headed down this course.

### Yazid's Commands

There are many other reasons to believe that the massacre at Karbala was only perpetrated by Yazid's command. For one, Yazid had a deep animus against Imam Hussain. After all, Imam Hussain was an adamant opponent of Muawiya's attempts to install Yazid as his successor.[21] Muawiya did not pursue the same tactics he had used against other opponents. Whenever Yazid advised his father to take a harsher stance against Imam Hussain, Muawiya would refuse despite Yazid's insistence. That agitated Yazid even more.[22]

Immediately after the death of Muawiya, Yazid moved to seize people's allegiance and was not willing to compromise with anyone. He had commanded his governor over Medina

---

[20] Ibn Al-Atheer, *Al-Kamil fi Al-Tareekh*, 4:306.

[21] Al-Tabari, *Tareekh Al-Tabari*, 4:226.

[22] Ibn Asakir, *Tareekh Dimashq*, 14:206.

to call Imam Hussain, Abdullah ibn Omar, Abdulrahman ibn Abu Bakr, and Abdullah ibn Al-Zubayr for their allegiance. Yazid made the specific order that if any of these men refused to give allegiance, then they are to be decapitated and their heads are to be sent to Damascus.[23]

In another letter to Abdullah ibn Abbas, Yazid wrote, "Your cousin, Hussain, and the enemy of God, ibn Al-Zubayr, have refused to give me allegiance, are causing sedition in Mecca, and have subjected themselves to grave danger."[24] There are even reports that Yazid had sent assassins to Mecca to make sure that Imam Hussain's movement does not spread.[25]

Yazid's actions after the massacre of Karbala are equally telling. He commanded ibn Ziyad to send the captives, along with the decapitated heads of the martyrs to Damascus. The women and children were marched in shackles as the severed heads of their loved ones loomed over them from Iraq to Syria. Once they reached Damascus, Yazid commanded the head of Imam Hussain be displayed in front of his palace for three days.[26] He was outwardly jubilant and would sing poetry in the stupor of his victory.

And if there is any doubt that Yazid did not issue the command for the massacre, would he keep an insubordinate general such as ibn Ziyad as the governor of Kufa? In fact,

---

[23] Ibn A'tham, *Al-Futuh*, 5:9.
[24] Sibt ibn Al-Jawzi, *Tathkirat Al-Khawas*, 237-38.
[25] Al-Qunduzi, *Yanabee' Al-Mawadda*, 3:59.
[26] Ibn Asakir, *Tareekh Dimashq*, 69:160.

history tells us that Yazid honored and rewarded ibn Ziyad for his deeds.[27]

And if Yazid was of the type that would repent after such a massacre, would he allow a similar massacre to take place in Medina only a year later? And would he allow for the siege of Mecca and the demolishing of part of the Grand Mosque?

## *Evading Responsibility*

Nevertheless, some historians claim that Yazid denounced the massacre or disclaimed any responsibility for the battle. Some historians say that he shifted the blame to ibn Ziyad.[28] Others claim that his family joined Imam Hussain's family in mourning.[29]

No one would deny that he hastily allowed the family of Imam Hussain to return to Medina. And that he allowed them to mourn freely. Even when the revolt in Medina occurred a year later, he commanded his men not to lay a hand on Imam Ali ibn Hussain.[30] He even excused him from having to pay allegiance[31] where everyone else was forced to profess that they were 'slaves of Yazid.'[32]

But with all the evidence that we have mentioned showing that Yazid was in fact behind the massacre, the most that this could mean is that he was trying to evade responsibility.

---

[27] Ibn A'tham, *Al-Futuh*, 5:156.

[28] Ibn Al-Atheer, *Al-Kamil Fi Al-Tareekh*, 4:84-7.

[29] Al-Tabari, *Tareekh Al-Tabari*, 4:355.

[30] Al-Dhahabi, *Siyar A'lam Al-Nubala*, 3:320.

[31] Al-Tabari, *Tareekh Al-Tabari*, 4:379.

[32] Al-Asqalani, *Al-Isaba*, 6:232.

This shouldn't come as a surprise, especially in the wake of the mounting public sentiment against Umayyad tyranny.

As ibn Al-Atheer writes in his historical account,

> *When the severed head of Hussain reached Yazid, ibn Ziyad's status rose in his court. He was overjoyed by [ibn Ziyad's] actions and rewarded him. It was not long before news of people's hatred reached [Yazid], and how they would curse and damn him. Thus he began to regret the murder of Hussain. He would say, '... May God curse [ibn Ziyad]! He coerced [Hussain to fight] and killed him. Through that, he vilified me in the eyes of the Muslims...'[33]*

Ibn Ziyad was also looking to evade responsibility for the massacre. Instead, he wanted to shift responsibility to Omar ibn Saad. He demanded from Omar ibn Saad to hand back the letter that he had sent him issuing the command for killing Imam Hussain. But Omar was on to ibn Ziyad's ruse and refused to hand over the letter, claiming that it was lost. He kept it as proof that the command to kill Imam Hussain came from his superiors.[34]

Even ibn Ziyad's mother, Marjana, would chide her son, saying, "You wretched man! You killed the grandson of the Messenger of God! You will never set eyes on Paradise."[35]

Yazid and ibn Ziyad's efforts to evade responsibility were so great, that it reflected in their handling of other situations. Although it did not stop them from perpetrating more

---

[33] Ibn Al-Atheer, *Al-Kamil Fi Al-Tareekh*, 4:87.

[34] Al-Tabari, *Tareekh Al-Tabari*, 4:357.

[35] Ibn A'tham, *Al-Futuh*, 5:174.

crimes, they became wearier of how their image would be affected.

Yazid was adamant that Abdullah ibn Al-Zubayr must be subjected to Umayyad rule. But he hesitated and tried to temper his response. He would say to his courtiers,

> *Woe to you! Yesterday I killed Hussain ibn Ali, and now [you ask me to] kill Abdullah ibn Al-Zubayr? I fear that my subjects will be divided against me and that they will not tolerate this from me.*[36]

Despite his initial hesitations, Yazid made a decision and commanded ibn Ziyad to set siege to Mecca. But ibn Ziyad refused, saying, "I shall not combine these two acts for the sake of this wretch. Would I kill the grandson of the Prophet and set siege to the Grand Mosque [for him]?"[37]

This is generally the way that politicians react when they realize the errors of their policies. They attempt to shift the blame for their wrongdoings onto others in order to avoid public backlash. Sometimes, they would try to pin things on their underlings, claiming that they had no knowledge of their actions. At other times, they would shift the blame to their superiors, claiming that they had no choice but to follow their commands.

Thus, we see that Omar ibn Saad attempted to pin the blame on Yazid and ibn Ziyad. Ibn Ziyad in turn attempted to shift blame away from himself and pin it on Omar ibn Saad and Yazid. Yazid could have done the same with ibn Ziyad, specifically when it came to the crimes committed at

---

[36] Ibn A'tham, *Al-Futuh*, 5:174.

[37] Al-Tabari, *Tareekh Al-Tabari*, 4:371.

Karbala. However, it seems that Yazid's pleasure with ibn Ziyad's actions did not allow him to adequately shift the blame away from himself. He flagrantly showed his joy and did not take any action against ibn Ziyad during the remainder of his reign.

*Folly of the Crime*

It seems that Al-Waleed ibn Utba, Yazid's governor over Medina, realized the folly of this great crime. From the onset, he refused to lay a hand on Imam Hussain. Yazid eventually removed him for his insubordination.[38]

Muawiya had realized this as well. That might be why, as some historians recount, Muawiya advised his son Yazid not to harm Imam Hussain. Al-Tabari writes that Muawiya told his son Yazid,

> *As for Hussain ibn Ali, the people of Iraq will not leave him until he rises. If he does so and you put down his rebellion, be clement with him. He is of a noteworthy lineage and bears a great right.[39]*

Yet Muawiya himself had poisoned Imam Hussain's brother, Imam Hassan.[40] Muawiya outwardly celebrated Imam Hassan's death[41] despite the same lineage and right that he holds.

Even Abdulmalik ibn Marwan, whose father was known for his animosity against the Alids, realized the folly of the crimes at Karbala. Marwan was amongst the agitators that

---

[38] Al-Qurtubi, *Al-Isti'ab*, 3:1388.

[39] Al-Tabari, *Tareekh Al-Tabari*, 4:238.

[40] Al-Qurtubi, *Al-Isti'ab*, 1:389.

[41] Al-Daynouri, *Al-Imama wa Al-Siyasa*, 1:142.

ensured Imam Hussain's murder. But when his son took the throne, he wrote to his governor in Hijaz, Al-Hajjaj Al-Thaqafi, "Avoid the blood of the family of [Ali ibn] Abu Talib, for I saw how the reign of the children of Harb[42] ended when they killed Hussain."[43]

Yazid did not stop at the killing of Imam Hussain, but followed the massacre with another massacre in Medina and by setting siege to the Grand Mosque. So why does Abdulmalik ibn Marwan only cite the massacre of Karbala as the reason for the doom of that part of the Umayyad dynasty?

It seems that Abdulmalik realized as well the great folly of the crimes committed in Karbala and that no other tragedy is comparable in weight.

---

[42] The children of Harb is a reference to Mauwiya, Yazid, and Muawiya II, who were descendants of Abu Sufyan ibn Harb ibn Umayya. They were the only caliphs from that side of the Umayyad family. The remainder of the caliphs of the Umayyad dynasty were Marwan ibn Al-Hakam ibn Abu Al-Aas ibn Umayya and his descendants. This branch of the Umayyad family is also referred to as the Marwanites. –Eds.
[43] Al-Bayhaqi, *Al-Mahasin*, 40.

# THE FRUITS OF TRAGEDY

The first and foremost priority of Imam Hussain was to safeguard the religion of Islam. In dedication to this mission, he would cross any obstacle and overcome any hardship.

We revere Imam Hussain not only because of his courage, sense of justice, patience, fortitude, or sacrifice. We revere him because of the principles he stood for and the mission that he accomplished. We admire these qualities in him not just for their independent value, but because he utilized them in service of his mission. He utilized these traits to fulfill his obligation toward the religion with utmost sincerity.

Imam Hussain unconditionally accepted his role as the guardian of the religion. He did everything in his power to live up to that responsibility and fulfill his mission. When that mission required that he wait out Muawiya's reign despite his wicked nature, he did so. And when his mission required that he make his stance with full knowledge of the tragic outcome, he did not hesitate to rise to the occasion.

As we discussed previously, Imam Hussain's uprising was the culmination of a divine plan. Therefore, the goal of such uprising must be religious in nature. The goal must also be so significant that it warrants such a great sacrifice on the part of Imam Hussain, his family and companions. Through this line of reasoning, Shia scholars have concluded that the ultimate goal of Imam Hussain's movement was the protection of the faith.

What remains to be discussed are the details of how Imam Hussain was able to preserve the faith through his sacrifice and the threat that required him to set out on this journey.

## What did Imam Hussain Achieve?

It is clear that Imam Hussain's uprising and sacrifice did not mean an end to dynastic and hereditary rule in the Muslim nation. The caliphate continued to be determined by power and bloodline, rather than virtue and competence, even after the massacre at Karbala.

And even though some had protested Muawiya's attempts to establish dynastic rule through his bloodline, the Muslim nation quickly acclimated itself to the new reality. Muslim scholars even began to issue verdicts that legitimized such hereditary rule.

Moreover, the tragedy at Karbala only increased Umayyad bloodlust, as they became accustomed to constant bloodshed. Imam Hussain's rise did not stop succeeding generations of Muslim rulers from engaging in unbridled oppression and transgression in the name of Islam. It did not protect the Muslim nation from disunity and civil strife either.

It is not farfetched to think that had the Umayyad clan faced a situation similar to what happened in Karbala, they would not be able to avoid their previous mistakes. In fact, they may even find a way to intensify their crimes and transgression in a similar situation.

One may even argue that the events of the massacre had only deepened the schism between the followers of the Alid line and the rest of the Muslims – between Shia and Sunni Muslims. The result was a great deal of violence, bloodshed, and transgression.

Nor did it stop the degeneration of the Muslim nation religiously and morally. It did not stop the surge in drinking, gambling, fraud, promiscuity, and disregard for human life.

Why then? Despite all this, we know that the mission that Imam Hussain set out to accomplish was far greater than to be outweighed by these factors. His mission was indeed so great that it was worthy of the sacrifices given by him, his family, and his companions. We set out in this book in an attempt to discern and evaluate the gains of Imam Hussain's movement and sacrifice.

## PRESERVING THE FAITH

If we look at the heritage of Prophet Muhammad's Progeny, we find that they put a great emphasis on the tragedy of Imam Hussain. They instructed their followers to commemorate the tragedy and remember the sacrifice. But the same emphasis was not given to the question of why the sacrifice was made in the first place.

If we go back to the words of Imam Hussain, we see that he had aimed to achieve a great 'victory' through his sacrifice. His son, Imam Ali Zayn Al-Abideen, alluded that the simple fact that prayer continued to be held was a measure of the victory of Imam Hussain's uprising.

But still, they did not clarify the meaning of this victory and why such a sacrifice had to be made.

*In His Visitation*

In one of the visitations[1] of Imam Hussain, as narrated by Imam Jafar al-Sadiq, we read,

> *He [i.e. Imam Hussain] has fulfilled his obligation through his calls [to You, oh God]. He sacrificed his life for You. All that so he can rescue Your servants from deviance, ignorance, blindness, doubt, and uncertainty – towards the gates of guidance and away from ruination.*[2]

In another visitation, al-Sadiq also says,

> *He [i.e. Imam Hussain] has fulfilled his obligation through his calls [to You, oh God]. He offered advice [to Your servants] and sacrificed his life for You. All that so he can rescue Your servants from ignorance and the bewilderment of deviance.*[3]

These passages are clear in indicating that the goal of Imam Hussain's uprising was to introduce people to the religion in its true and untarnished form. He wished to clarify its teach-

---

[1] A visitation, or *Ziyara*, is a form of supplication whereby an individual sends his salutations to the Prophet Muhammad, the Immaculate Imams, and other Muslim figures who hold a great status in the eyes of God. –Eds.

[2] Al-Qummi, *Kamil Al-Ziyarat*, 401.

[3] Al-Tousi, *Misbah Al-Mutahajjid*, 788.

ings. He wished to remove confusion about the reality of the message of his grandfather Prophet Muhammad, even if the majority of the people were unwilling to follow that message.

And this may be the same meaning that Lady Zainab refers to when she stood in the court of Yazid and delivered her famous speech. After seeing Yazid hit Imam Hussain's severed head with a cane, she said,

> *Plot as you wish. Continue with your undertakings. Exert all your efforts. But, by God, you will never erase our remembrance. You will never kill our inspiration. You will never reach our stature.*[4]

This is a clear indication that the message of Islam was in grave danger of being altered or dismantled. Through his sacrifice, Imam Hussain was able to change that. He was able to protect the faith from alteration and make clear to all who could see what the true teachings of the Prophet were.

This goal is one of the greatest aims of God's divine plan. God the Almighty wishes to clarify to us the teachings of our faith and set a proof upon us so that we cannot be justified in deviating from His word. "So that he who perishes might perish by a manifest proof, and he who lives may live on by a manifest proof."[5]

God says, "God does not lead any people astray after He has guided them until He has made clear to them what they should beware of."[6]

---

[4] Al-Khawarizmi, *Maqtal Al-Hussain*, 63-64.
[5] The Holy Quran, 8:42.
[6] The Holy Quran, 9:115.

He also says, "We do not punish [any community] until We have sent [it] an apostle"[7] – "so that mankind may not have any argument against God, after the [sending of the] apostles."[8]

Imam Hussain's sacrifice was not the only thing that protected Islam from being completely altered or dismantled. In fact, Islam had two special qualities that ensured its preservation.

Firstly, God revealed to His Prophet a book – the Holy Quran – that is accepted by all Muslims and has been safeguarded from any alteration.

Secondly, God granted the religion a corps of dedicated guardians to the faith – twelve immaculate leaders from the family of the Holy Prophet. When they were deprived of their rights and disallowed to practice the full authority that they were given, Islam came under a grave danger of being altered or dismantled. But God the Almighty entrusted the Progeny of His Messenger with the duty of preserving the faith, and they did so despite all adversity.

They persisted in their mission to clarify the tenets of God's religion. They were God's proof upon His servants. They persevered against all odds and all enemies, especially the succeeding tyrannical dynasties that ruled in the name of the faith. They complemented each other's efforts in this regard, each of them acting according to the dictates of his circumstances. Through this, they fulfilled God's divine mission with the utmost excellence.

---

[7] The Holy Quran, 17:15.
[8] The Holy Quran, 4:165.

The reality of the matter is that Imam Hussain's sacrifice had the greatest effect in this regard, as we will discuss later in this book.

So what does preserving the faith entail?

To preserve the tenets of the religion as God revealed them unto the Prophet, two things must remain true. Firstly, there must always be an undisputed religious authority so that it can clarify any confusion regarding God's revelation. Secondly, there must be a group of individuals who call unto the truth and remind the heedless – without that, the true tenets of the religion would be abandoned.

Imam Hussain's sacrifice had a great effect in establishing both of those requirements. This will become clearer as we continue through this book.

# FABRICATIONS

God the Almighty sent messengers to mankind to guide them and help them towards the path of excellence. Each of these messages must be preserved until it is superseded by another message. Throughout the lifetime of each message, there must be ample invitation towards the message and clarification of its tenets – "So that he who perishes might perish by a manifest proof, and he who lives may live on by a manifest proof."[1]

The preservation of the message can only be ensured if the guardian of the faith, appointed by God Almighty, is immaculate in nature. This would guarantee that whoever is given the mission of preserving the faith does not fall short of God's divine will. This was the case with all previous messages, as is confirmed by the narrations of our Holy Prophet and his Progeny.

Yet we see that all religions were afflicted by some form of disagreement after the passing of their messenger or prophet. And it is usually the case, except in rare circumstances,

---

[1] The Holy Quran, 8:42.

that the side of evil and deviance has the upper hand in these disputes.

Why? It is because the side of good — the side of the immaculate guardian appointed by God — is always restrained by principles and values that cannot be compromised. As Imam Hussain said,

> *People are slaves of this world, and religion is only words on their tongues. They use it in whichever way they can to secure a living for themselves. If they are prodded with tribulation the true believers will be less.*[2]

The faithful will not pursue deviant ploys and vile means to reach their goals. They are bound by principles and will not steer away from the path of righteousness and truth. But this is a weakness in this materialistic world. The wicked realize this and use it against God's servants. With their trickery, they achieve a limited worldly victory for themselves. As Imam Ali says,

> *One who has experienced the thick and thin of life [can easily find] a way to trick [and deceive]. Yet he is prevented [from utilizing these ploys and deceptions] by God's commands and prohibitions. So he disregards [utilizing these ploys] after having identified them and despite his capability to utilize them]. While one who has no restraints of religion seizes the opportunity [in disregard to God's commands].*[3]

---

[2] Al-Khawarizmi, *Maqtal Al-Hussain*, 1:236.
[3] Al-Radi, *Nahj Al-Balagha*, 1:92, Sermon 41.

## DECEPTIVE VICTORIES

This may be the reason why the deviants tend to emerge victorious whenever a nation becomes mired in disputes after the passing of its prophet.[4] They utilize the name of religion to serve their own whims and ends. By this, they try to alter the faith's tenets to fit their own interests. And with power and authority in their grasp, they often succeeded.

The source of alteration, fabrication, and deviation in the religion thus stems from the political authority that lies in the hands of these deviant forces. They attempt to twist the religion to support and expand their political ambitions.

Yet God has made it incumbent upon Himself to clarify the tenets of faith and set clear proof for the path of truth. That is because He does not punish without setting a clear standard. In addition, He has given us a religion by His wisdom, and that wisdom would not be fulfilled if the religion were not clearly delivered to mankind.

Therefore, any victory for evil against the side of good must be in a way that does not completely deface the truth or eradicate the message. There must always be a manifest proof in support of the truth.

Any deviation away from the truth is therefore not due to any fault or deficiency in it. Rather, whoever chooses to go against the truth does so with full knowledge and takes full responsibility. As God Almighty says, "Indeed, with God religion is Islam, and those who were given the Book did

---

4 Al-Haythami, *Majma' Al-Zawaed*, 1:157.

not differ except after knowledge had come to them, out of envy among themselves."[5]

Of course, this only applies to the message and religion that God wishes to remain in effect. As for any religion that has been supplanted or superseded by another message, such a manifest proof is not necessary. A person will only be justified in following the religion that God wishes him to follow, and will not be justified in following a message that has been superseded. Therefore, the fact that the details of past divine messages have been lost or altered does not harm our analysis here.

This is why Islam is different from all previous messages. Since the message of Islam is eternal and will remain so long as mankind inhabits the Earth, there must always be a manifest proof of its teachings.

With the grace of God, the efforts of the Household of the Prophet whom God had appointed as the guardians of the faith are the manifest proof for its teachings. Imam Hussain's sacrifice had the greatest impact in this regard, as we hope to explain further throughout this book.

We also hope to explain why this grave danger that faced Islam was not simply Yazid's government or the deception of the Umayyad clan. Yes, these things had exacerbated the danger and made the sacrifice more urgent, but nonetheless there were greater dangers at play.

---

[5] The Holy Quan, 3:19.

# IMMACULATE GUARDIANS

The immaculate guardians of the faith appointed by God are the Twelve Immaculate Imams from the Household of the Prophet, starting with the Commander of the Faithful Imam Ali ibn Abu Talib, and ending with the Twelfth Holy Imam Muhammad ibn Al-Hassan Al-Mahdi (aj).[6] The proof of this is beyond the scope of this book and is left for the books of theology.

This has a number of important implications for our study. The Prophet has told us that it is an obligation for us to come to know the Imam of our time – "Whoever dies without knowing the Imam of his time dies the death of the Age of Ignorance."[7]

We are also obligated to follow the commands of these Imams. God says in His Holy Book, "O you who have faith! Obey God and obey the Apostle and those vested with authority among you."[8]

In addition, we are obligated to hold tight to their guidance in unity as a nation. God says, "Hold fast, all together, to God's cord, and do not be divided."[9]

---

[6] The abbreviation "aj" stands for *Ajjalallah Farajah*, which is a short prayer asking God to hasten the reappearance of the Awaited Mahdi. – Eds.

[7] Al-Sadouq, *Kamal Al-Deen*, 409. The "Age of Ignorance" is a term that refers to the era predating the message of the Prophet Muhammad. – Eds.

[8] The Holy Quran, 4:59. The ones who are "vested with authority" are the Immaculate Imams from the lineage of Prophet Muhammad, as is evident from the many narrations in this regard. –Eds.

[9] The Holy Quran, 3:103.

Thus, if these immaculate individuals were not deprived of their right and allowed to fulfill their rightful role as the leaders of the Muslim nation, they would have been able to lead the nation to unimaginable heights. For one, their immaculate character cannot be doubted. And with the textual exhortations to follow these divinely appointed guides, there would be no room to debate the legitimacy of their authority.

This is what Lady Fatima alluded to when she said in one of her sermons,

> By God, if they divert away from the manifest way and did not accept the clear proof, he [i.e. Imam Ali] would bring them back toward [the way] and charged them with [the clear proof]. He would have led them with ease, treading lightly along the way such that his followers do not grow tired. He would have led them to a spring – luminous, pure, and quenching – plentifully gushing, but not overflowing. He would have fed them until they grew plump. He would have counseled them in private and in public.[10]

Indeed, had the nation followed the path of God's divinely appointed leaders, it would have indulged much more lavishly in the luxury of God's blessings. God says in the Holy Quran, "If the people of the towns had been faithful and God-wary, We would have opened to them blessings from the heaven and the earth."[11]

But the nation diverted away from the commands of God and His Prophet. They oppressed the Household of the

---

[10] Ibn Tayfour, *Balaghat Al-Nisa*, 19-20.
[11] The Holy Quran, 7:96.

Prophet and robbed them of their rights instead of allowing them the position of authority that God had ordained for them. The nation chose to go its own way and settle on a system where political authority was vested in whoever most effectively wielded force and deception.

## Ardent Opposition and Reluctant Support

Imam Ali and Lady Fatima decried this wretched course that the nation chose to take. They set out to remind the people that they must obey the commands of God and the teachings of His Prophet. Yet they did not heed their words and they continued on the course they had taken.

Still, Imam Ali had to maintain stability within the situation that the nation chose so as not to break the back of the young Muslim community. He had to preserve his own life and the life of his followers so that they could safeguard the message of the Messenger.

The newly founded political power of the caliphate set out to expand its domain and conquer nearby lands. Soon, the Muslim nation had expanded over large swaths of territories. The nation grew in stature, dominion, and influence and was no longer a young and fragile community. But the Islam that expanded was not the same Islam that the Prophet had preached. Instead the Islam that spread was one propagated by political and military authorities using the sword. This distorted version of Islam held the political leader – the caliph – as the supreme symbol of faith regardless of his actions and character.

Imam Ali had reluctantly supported the political authority of the time – not because it had any legitimacy or because its actions were justified, but because safeguarding the faith required such support. In a letter to the people of Egypt years later, he wrote,

> I was dismayed when I saw that the people had assembled to give allegiance to so-and-so. But I stayed my hand until I saw that people began to reject Islam and call for the decimation of the religion of Muhammad. I feared that if I did not support Islam and the Muslims I would soon see the faith severed or demolished. That would have been a tragedy greater than the loss of your government. I rose in those circumstances until falsity was removed and defeated, and until faith was safeguarded and relieved.[12]

## Means of Fabrication

The political rulers of the state took a number of gravely dangerous steps in order to solidify their rule and create a false legitimacy for their dynasties.

### Usurped Titles

The political establishment that followed the death of the Prophet began to use words and symbols that gave them a religious aura. They would call the ruler of the Muslim nation the 'caliph' – or successor – of the Prophet. They would also use titles such as 'Commander of the Faithful' and 'Vicegerent of the Prophet.' The first three caliphs even used the ring of the Prophet to seal their letters. The first two were buried beside the Prophet.

---

[12] Al-Radi, *Nahj Al-Balagha*, 3:119.

The trend continued and the caliphs became so haughty that they insisted on people calling them by titles such as 'the Vicegerent of God' and 'God's Authority on Earth.'

It is ironic that the religious scholars that supported this view did not come up with any compelling theory that legitimized the government in a way that would warrant these titles. The most widely adopted theories allowed legitimacy to be obtained by the sword or through hereditary right – neither of which would warrant a title that would attribute the ruler's position to a divine or prophetic nature.

This was evident from the outset of the creation of the state after the death of the Prophet. In a long conversation between the first caliph and Abbas, the Prophet's uncle, Abbas says, "How distant is the title you take as the successor of the Messenger of God, from your claim that people were left to choose and chose you."[13]

Imam Ali made a similar argument in those formative years after the Prophet's death. When people called him to give allegiance to the first caliph and said, 'the successor of the Messenger of God calls you forth.' Imam Ali responded, "How quickly you have fabricated against the Messenger of God!"[14]

**Imam Ali and the Title of 'Commander of the Faithful'**

The succeeding caliphs of the state tried their best to usurp the title of 'Commander of the Faithful.' The title was not only an eloquent honorific, but was also a unique epithet given to one of their rivals.

---

[13] Al-Yaqoubi, *Tareekh Al-Yaqoubi*, 2:125.
[14] Al-Daynouri, *Al-Imama wa Al-Siyasa*, 1:16.

'Commander of the Faithful' was a title reserved for Imam Ali ibn Abu Talib. This fact is not only evident from the narrations of the Holy Household,[15] but is also supported by textual evidence accepted by other schools of thought.[16] The Prophet was known to use the title in reference to Imam Ali on multiple occasions.[17] It is even narrated that it is a title given to Imam Ali by God and delivered to him by Gabriel,[18] and that God would call him by this title on Judgment Day.[19]

*Restricting Narration*

The ruling authorities also aimed to strengthen their rule by restricting the narration of traditions relayed by the companions of the Prophet. The writing down of traditions was forbidden by the government in the formative years of Islam.[20] Anything that was written down was burned.[21]

People were only allowed to narrate the traditions of the Prophet that were agreeable to the rulers' interests. The rulers became so perverse that they imprisoned the companion Abu Thar for the alleged crime of fabrication.[22] Abu Thar was known for his honesty and was praised by the Prophet who said, "Trees have not shaded and sands have not carried a speaker more truthful than Abu Thar."[23]

---

[15] See, for example: Al-Kulayni, *Al-Kafi*, 1:411.
[16] See, for example: Al-Khawarizmi, *Al-Manaqib*, 303.
[17] See, for example: Ibn Asakir, *Tareekh Dimashq*, 42:306, 326, 328, 368.
[18] Al-Khawarizmi, *Al-Manaqib*, 323.
[19] Ibn Asakir, *Tareekh Dimashq*, 42:326.
[20] Ibn Abdulbar, *Jami' Bayan Al-Ilm*, 1:65.
[21] Al-Dhahabi, *Tathkirat Al-Hoffadh*, 1:65.
[22] Al-Dhahabi, *Tathkirat Al-Hoffadh*, 1:7.
[23] Al-Shaybani, *Musnad Ahmad*, 5:197.

The government was brutal in the implementation of this policy. Companions would be so fearful of conveying narrations that went against the government that they often told their disciples not to publicize them. In one instance, a companion fell ill and so he told one of his disciples, "I will share with you narrations that God may allow you to benefit from in the future. If I live, do not attribute this to me. If I die, then you can spread them as you wish for I will be in a safe place."[24]

The scope of these restrictions did not stop at relaying narrations, but seem to have extended to learning in general. It is well documented that a man by the name of Sabeegh came to Medina and asked about some verses of the Quran, for which the second caliph actually punished him. Some historians say that he was beaten severely.[25] Others say that the Muslims were forbidden from accompanying him[26] or visiting him in his illness.[27] Furthermore, some accounts relay that his rations and livelihood were cut off.[28]

## Omar's Character

Such accounts do not come as a surprise, especially knowing Omar's aggressive nature. Many people protested Abu Bakr's appointment of Omar as successor. For example, one companion told Abu Bakr regarding this, "What would you say to your lord [on Judgment Day] when you have giv-

---

[24] Al-Nisaburi, *Sahih Muslim*, 4:48.
[25] Al-Darimi, *Sunan Al-Darimi*, 1:54.
[26] Al-Darimi, *Sunan Al-Darimi*, 1:54.
[27] Al-Siyouti, *Al-Durr Al-Manthoor*, 2:7.
[28] Ibn Asakir, *Tareekh Dimashq*, 23:413.

en authority to a harsh and hardhearted man? People are repelled from him and hearts are repulsed by him."[29]

 And when people complained about the policies of Omar's successor, Othman, he would say, "You have disparaged me for things and hated policies that you endured under [Omar]. But he had tightened the reigns and repressed you, so that you did not dare look at him [in contempt] or point to him [in reproach]."[30]

And when Imam Ali was chosen by the people as the fourth caliph, he described Omar saying,

> [The first caliph] entrusted the matter to a dominion of a haughty tone and a rough touch. Its mistakes were plenty, and so were its excuses. One in contact with it was like the rider of an unruly camel – if he tugged on its rein the very nostril would be slit, but if he let it loose he would be flung off its back. And so, by God, the people were tried with recklessness, wickedness, unsteadiness, and deviation. Nevertheless, I remained patient despite the length of the period and the difficulty of the trial.[31]

## Lies and Fabrications

No less dangerous were the lies that were fabricated against the Prophet so that they could alter the religion to what suits their interests. Imam Ali has beautiful words in this regard. When a man approached him and asked about the contradictions between narrations and whether there was any fabrication in the traditions, he said,

[29] Al-Mutazili, *Sharh Nahj Al-Balagha*, 1:164.
[30] Al-Daynouri, *Al-Imama wa Al-Siyasa*, 1:28.
[31] Al-Radi, *Nahj Al-Balagha*, 1:33.

*You have asked, so comprehend this answer. In the hands of the people there is truth and falsity, facts and lies – narrations that are abrogating and abrogated, general and specific, definitive and metaphorical, and correct and incorrect. People have attributed fabrications to the Messenger of God when he was alive, and so he gave a sermon in which he said, 'Oh people! There have been many liars fabricating about me. Know that whoever deliberately lies about me, let him prepare for his seat in hellfire.' Nonetheless, people lied about him after his death.*

*Know that whatever is relayed to you comes from one of four types of people – there is no fifth to them:*

*[It may come from] a hypocrite who shows faith and exhibits Islam, but does not fear sinning and is unashamed of lying about the Messenger of God deliberately. If people knew that he was a lying hypocrite, they would not accept his word or believe him. However, they say, 'He accompanied the Messenger of God. He saw him and heard his words.' They thus take his word without knowing the reality of his case... [These hypocrites] grew near to the leaders of deviance and callers unto hellfire through their fabrications, lies, and slander. For this, they were given office and authority over people's lives. They [the hypocrite governors] were used [by the Umayyads] to overtake the world. Yet people align with their kings and with the material world, except for those whom God has protected. This is the first of the four.*

*Another heard from the Messenger of God but did not understand and misquoted him, without deliberately lying...*

*A third heard a command of the Messenger of God which was later retraced, but he did not know of this retraction [or vice versa]...*

*The fourth never lied about the Messenger of God. He abhors dishonesty out of fear of God and respect for the Messenger of God. He did not forget, but memorized what he heard precisely and conveyed it accurately without adding or subtracting. He knew of what was abrogating and what was abrogated, so he worked according to the abrogating and rejected the abrogated.*

*The case of the Prophet is just like the Quran. There are [traditions that are] abrogating and abrogates, general and specific, and definitive and metaphorical. The Messenger of God may at times say things that have both a general and a specific meaning – just like the Quran. And God says in his book, 'Take whatever the Apostle gives you, and refrain from whatever he forbids you.'[32] But this could be misconstrued by anyone who did not know and realize what God and His Prophet meant.*

*And not every one of the companions would ask the Messenger of God and [fully] understand [the response]. There were some that would ask but would not comprehend. So much so that they would love for a nomad or a stranger to come and ask the Messenger of God so that they could listen.[33]*

Imam Ali also said,

*Where are those who claim that they – and not us – are the ones who are 'firmly grounded in knowledge'?[34] They have lied and transgressed against us, just because God has promoted us and demoted them, given us and withheld from*

---

[32] The Holy Quran, 59:7.
[33] Al-Kulayni, *Al-Kafi*, 1:62-64.
[34] Referencing: The Holy Quran, 3:7.

*them, and accepted us and rejected them. Through us guidance is sought. Through us blindness is cured.*[35]

## Enshrining Obedience

The political elites of the caliphate's state also focused their efforts on enshrining the concept of obedience in the minds of the people.

As we discussed previously, God had commanded us to know His divinely appointed guardians of faith. He commanded us to follow their commands and remain united on their path.

The political elites used these divine commands but transformed their meaning in the minds of the public. They used their propaganda machines to convince people that the subject matter of these commands – the people that must be followed – are not God's divinely appointed vicegerents, but the political authorities of the time. Even worse, the caliphs of the state sought to usurp the title of divine vicegerency for themselves, claiming that they rule by the will and command of God.

The perversity of these monarchs grew with succeeding generations. The Abbasid caliphs had based their revolution against the Umayyad dynasty on the premise that the Umayyad reign was illegitimate and that sovereignty must be in the hands of the Hashemite clan, of whom the Abbasids were descendants. These same Abbasid caliphs went on to legitimize the Umayyad dynasty and justify the acquisition of authority through force. They sought to once again enshrine the ideas of obedience to the ruler and vilify dissent.

---

[35] Al-Radi, *Nahj Al-Balagha*, 2:27.

After all, these ideas were integral to ensuring the establishment and permanence of the dynasties of the time.

These tactics pursued by the Umayyad and Abbasid dynasties had a toll on the outlook of the Muslim public. They instilled in the minds of the masses the idea that the regime is the legitimate representative of God on Earth. Any dissent by the people to that government would be religiously and morally inexcusable. This was especially evident in areas of the Muslim nation where the government had the greatest control, such as the Levant during Umayyad reign.

This ideology was propagated by successive governments by way of numerous tactics – including the fabrication of prophetic traditions. An example of this is the alleged narration that states, "Whoever sees something they abhor from their prince, let him be patient. Whoever leaves the fold of unity for the span of a palm and then dies, he has surely faced the death of the Age of Ignorance."[36]

In this, they fell in the same error as some early Christians when they interpreted the following passage of the scripture,

> Let every soul be subject unto the higher powers. For there is no power but of God: the powers that be are ordained of God. Whosoever therefore resisteth the power, resisteth the ordinance of God: and they that resist shall receive to themselves damnation. For rulers are not a terror to good works, but to the evil....[37]

---

[36] Al-Bukhari, *Sahih Al-Bukhari*, 8:87.
[37] Rom 13:1-3 KJV.

On the other hand, we see that Imam Ali would say in his sermons,

> *Oh people! I have some rights over you, as you have some rights over me. As for your right over me, it is that I give you fair counsel, safeguard your livelihoods, to educate you so that you do not become ignorant, and to discipline you to follow these teachings. As for my rights over you, it is that you are true to your oath of allegiance, to counsel me in private and in public, to answer me when I call unto you, and to obey when I command you.[38]*

According to Imam Ali's teachings, government is just another form of social contract – all parties are bound to follow through with their obligations. The governor is bound to dutifully perform the responsibilities of government, while the public is bound to obey the law and support a just governor.

Yet, God's commands for people to follow His divinely appointed vicegerent and to be united in the way of the truth were distorted. The caliphs took these commands out of context and misrepresented God's will to pursue their own agendas. These misrepresentations were even used to attack some of God's chosen servants – Imam Ali, Lady Fatima, Imam Hassan, and Imam Hussain – and their followers.

They used these distortions to obstruct the path of truth and justice and to stop the household of the Prophet from spreading the true teachings of the faith. They fought Imam Ali, Imam Hassan, and Imam Hussain to stop them from threatening their positions of power and influence, which,

---

[38] Al-Radi, *Nahj Al-Balagha*, 1:84.

in essence, was stopping them from enjoining good and forbidding evil.

Some refer to the notion of unity and its utmost significance. Of course, unity is an objective that should be worked for, aspired to, and attained. But unity must be for the sake of the truth and a higher purpose. To be united for the mere sake of unity is meaningless without a driving purpose towards the path of truth. In fact, if unity is achieved in pursuit of evil and wretched goals that would be abhorred. Instead, disunity in such a circumstance would be definitely more preferable because at least in the end there are some who are still pursuing justice and truth.

*Hypocrite Lackeys*

The governing authority also utilized the hypocrites amongst the public and the tribal chieftains as the pillars of their government. They became governors, viceroys, and army generals. They were given authority over people's lives and livelihood. These individuals did not hold and honor nobility. Rather, they used the political authority that was granted to them by the ruling elites to strike fear and false respect in the hearts of the people.

Thus, these individuals were in utmost need of the support of the caliph and his aides. They became blind followers of their superiors' commands and mindless executors of the caliph's will. They did all that is in their aim to strengthen the government, as it was the source of their power and prestige. They did not hesitate to comply with any order, no matter how wicked. They became the base of the state's expanding reach.

The second caliph rationalized this saying, "We will make use of the strength of the hypocrite, yet he [alone] will bear the weight of his sins."[39]

The second caliph would even let someone like Muawiya govern over the Levant without any intervention or management. He would even call Muawiya 'the Caesar of the Arabs.'[40]

In any case, it seems that these state policies led to the spread of hypocrisy across the lands. Aisha, the wife of the Messenger, mentions that hypocrisy took root in Medina after the death of the Prophet.[41] And not only did hypocrisy spread, but the hypocrites were not restrained or chided, but were given power and authority over others.

**Blaming Fate**

What made things even more complicated was that the individuals in power always blamed their actions on divine will. They always claimed that it was fate that led to their circumstance and predestination that made them act in the way they did.

Historical accounts mention a conversation between the second caliph and ibn Abbas. Omar complained to ibn Abbas, "Oh, ibn Abbas, I must complain to you of your cousin. I asked him to come with me but he refused. I still see him dismayed. What do you think is the matter?"

Ibn Abbas replied, "Surely you know."

"I think he is still distraught over the issue of the caliphate."

---

[39] Ibn Abu Shayba, *Al-Musannaf*, 7:269.

[40] Al-Qurtubi, *Al-Isti'ab*, 3:1417.

[41] Al-Bayhaqi, *Al-Sunan Al-Kubra*, 8:199.

"Yes, that is it. He claims that the Messenger wanted him to fill the role."

Omar could not contain his rage. "The Messenger wanted him to fill the role. So what if God the Almighty did not want that? The Messenger wanted something and God wanted something, so the will of God the Almighty overcame the will of His Messenger! Must every wish of the Messenger of God come to be?"[42]

The ruling authorities continued to use this as an excuse for their actions. They propagated the idea and, eventually, it was adopted by much of the public opinion.

## REVERBERATIONS

All this led to a great deal of fabrication and distortion that plagued the Muslim nation. Some would even say that, "Ali ibn Abu Talib reminded us of prayers that we used to pray with the Messenger of God but which we have either forgotten or abandoned intentionally."[43]

### Ignorant Muftis

In these circumstances, the guardians of the faith became the enemies of the state. The true teachings of Islam that they taught did not satisfy the ruling authority's interests. At the same time, the expansion of Muslim territory created a need for many more judges and religious guides.

---

[42] Al-Mutazili, *Sharh Nahj Al-Balagha*, 12:78-79.
[43] Al-Shaybani, *Musnad Ahmad*, 4:392.

This created a vacuum that the ruling authorities were quick to exploit. They began to appoint muftis[44] and judges without regard to knowledge and credentials. The only requirement was that the appointee was willing to follow the directives of the caliph and safeguard the interests of the regime.

This was the atmosphere in which fabrication and distortion grew. Muftis began to share contradicting views based on contradicting fabrications attributed to the Prophet. Judges contradicted one another; they neither knew the law nor were they willing to access to the keepers of the Prophet's knowledge. The positions of the state's clerical and judicial establishment became a matter of power and prestige, rather than being a vehicle for establishing justice and moral rectitude.

Imam Ali achingly described the circumstances:

> *When a problem is put before anyone of them he passes judgment solely based on his [unsupported] opinion. When exactly the same problem is placed before another of them he passes an opposite verdict. Then these judges go to the chief who had appointed them and he confirms all the verdicts, although their God is One, their Prophet is one, and their scripture is one!*
>
> *Is it that God ordered them to differ and they obeyed Him? Or He prohibited them from it but they disobeyed Him? Or that He sent an incomplete Faith and sought their help to complete it? Or were they His partners, so that they have the right to pronounce and He has to agree? Or is it that*

---

[44] Mufti: a government appointed scholar that is tasked with giving religious rulings. –Eds.

*God the Glorified sent a perfect faith but the Prophet fell short of conveying and delivering it?*

*But God the Glorified says, 'We have not omitted anything from the Book'[45] which contains 'clarification of all things.'[46] And He says that one part of the Quran verifies another part and that there is no divergence in it – He says, 'Had it been from [someone] other than God, they would have surely found much discrepancy in it.'[47]*

*Surely, what is apparent of the Quran is marvelous, while its latent [nuances] are profound. Its wonders will never end. Its amazements will never pass. Darkness will never be cleared except through it.[48]*

The ruling authorities did not care to clarify any standard for judgment. Without the guidance of the Prophet and his family, the Holy Book was not easily understood. It is no surprise that this led to carelessness in judgment, arrogance in opinion, and proliferation of controversy. All standards were lost.

Imam Ali lamented this state:

*Not everyone with a heart has intelligence. Not everyone capable of hearing can listen. Not everyone with sight can see. I'm awed – and why should I not be – at the errors of these sects and their arguments supporting their creed! They do not follow the traditions of a prophet, nor do they take the actions of a saint as an example. They do not believe in the unseen, nor do they chastise themselves from vice. They act*

---

[45] The Holy Quran, 6:38.

[46] The Holy Quran, 16:89.

[47] The Holy Quran, 4:82.

[48] Al-Radi, *Nahj Al-Balagha*, 1:54-55.

*on doubt and tread in [the way of] their desires. They con-*
*sider whatever they do to be good, and whatever they aban*
*don as evil.*

*Their reliance for resolving distress is on themselves. Their*
*confidence in regard to dubious matters is on their own opin-*
*ions, as if every one of them is his own religious guide.*
*Whatever he has decided himself he considers it to have been*
*taken through reliable sources and strong criteria.*[49]

The actions of the political elite in these formative years set the stage for the rise of religious sects and disunity amongst the Muslims. This started with the Kharijites and continues to this day. But the gravity of the circumstances of the early years of the Umayyad dynasty, lay in the fact that the opposition had yet to make its definitive stance.

In this environment, blasphemy and heresy became commonplace, and so did licentiousness and deviance. The teachings of Islam were either abandoned or distorted. People continued to follow the religion as dictated by their rulers, no matter how retched or wicked these chieftains were. An even larger portion of society did not care for the practical and moral teachings of any faith. Whatever was known of the religion was readily overlooked.

*Ending a False History*

History was also a focus of falsification and distortion. As we discussed earlier, titles were usurped and contrived in order to give the ruler fabricated legitimacy. The history and traditions of the Prophet were constantly being twisted so as to fit the rulers' aims.

---

[49] Al-Radi, *Nahj Al-Balagha*, 1:155-56.

This could have been exacerbated as the years passed on if it were allowed to continue. The nation was at a critical stage in which reform was crucial. Otherwise, the true teachings of the religion would have been distorted beyond recognition.

The Umayyad clan had come to power and set its foundation on false precepts and fabrications. The Levant, where they exercised complete control, did not know anything but Umayyad propaganda. Had the stage been cleared for them, they would have spread that throughout the nation. Had there not been a force of resistance, their reign would have been the end of Islam's true teachings and identity.

# IMAM ALI'S APPROACH

The conquests and expansion that the caliphate state pursued solidified the government's deviance and corruption. No one was willing to stand against a government that struck such awe in the hearts of the masses. Governors were able to use the spoils of war to buy the tongues and consciences of many. The restrictions that were placed on the true teachings of the Prophet and the distortions that the government propagated all led to the spread of ignorance and deviance across the nation.

Yet the caliphs' propaganda threatened to be their own downfall. They claimed that political authority was limited to the tribe of Quraysh, from whose bloodline the Prophet Muhammad descended. Yet they refuse to set any standard as to the character of the caliph or what clan of the Quraysh tribe he must hail from. This naturally led to a great deal of turmoil between the political elites. There were many companions of the Prophet that satisfied this requirement.

Envy began to brew amongst the chieftains of Quraysh. Omar's aggressive nature also led a group of these chieftains to dissent. In fact, Omar was so apprehensive of a ploy against him that when he was on his deathbed after an assassination attempt, he asked the chieftains of Quraysh, "Was this wound struck with your knowledge and deliberation?"[1]

Omar realized that so long as the Muslims were preoccupied with war and its spoils, they will not be tolerant to any change. Instead, they would have a vested interest in the continuity of the government and its status quo.

In order to keep the Muslims under the control of the government, Omar also realized that he needed to keep the most notable of the companions in Medina. They were not allowed to leave the city unless accompanied by strict surveillance.[2] By this, he made sure that they would not sow the seeds of dissent across the nation, especially since they were revered for the companionship of the Prophet. He justified his actions by asserting,

> *[The men of] Quraysh want to take the wealth of God as a means to their ends. Clearly, there are those amongst [the men of] Quraysh who harbor [hopes for] disunity and aspire to doff the shackles [of their oath of allegiance]. Surely, this will not happen so long as [I] remain alive.*[3]

At the same time, the Household of the Prophet realized the grave situation that had been created. The nation was still fragile and had to be dealt with carefully. Thus, the Prophet's Household refrained from claiming their right publically, but restricted that to only the most loyal of their companions. Through that, they insured that they were not the cause of division in the nation. They focused their ef-

---

[1] Al-San'ani, *Al-Musannaf*, 10:357.
[2] See: Al-Tabari, *Tareekh Al-Tabari*, 3:426.
[3] Al-Mutazili, *Sharh Nahj Al-Balagha*, 11:12.

forts squarely on preserving the true teachings of the Prophet.

The Household of the Prophet knew full well the reality of their circumstances. They realized the brutality of the caliphs and knew what the nation had turned to. Lady Fatima had warned against all this very soon after the death of the Prophet,

> *[The tree] has been fertilized, so wait until it gives its fruit! You will fill your cauldrons with newly spilt blood and deadly poison. On that day 'the falsifiers will fail'[4] and the wretched will realize the results of what their predecessors established. There, you must let yourselves be comforted away from this world and muster fortitude in the face of sedition. Give tidings to a piercing sword, the tyranny of a repressive aggressor, enveloping pandemonium, and despotism on the side of oppressors that will leave your livelihoods meager and your band an [easy] harvest.[5]*

## THE REIGN OF OTHMAN

At the beginning of Othman's reign, the caliphate's state had extended from Egypt to Persia. The Muslims were enamored with the power of their state and the spoils of its wars. They turned a blind eye to the usurpations of titles and the many aggressions of their rulers. Eventually, the idea of the caliph's divine authority became a widely spread view amongst the Muslim nation.

---

[4] The Holy Quran, 45:27.
[5] Ibn Tayfour, *Balaghat Al-Nisa*, 19-20.

Most importantly, the Muslims turned a blind eye to the bases of Othman's accession. Allegiance was given to Othman based on three conditions: that he follow the Quran, the tradition of the Prophet, and the precedent of the first two caliphs. The nation had become so enthralled by its rulers that it began to equate them to the Book of God and His Prophet!

All this was so that Imam Ali does not come to power. They knew that if he were to take his rightful place as the leader of the Muslim nation, he would establish justice and truth across the land and against their interest. Omar himself had said to Imam Ali, "Surely by God, if you were to be given authority over them, you would subject them to the evident truth and the clear path."[6]

In another historical account, Omar asked a chieftain of Quraysh who he would predict would be given the seat of succession. The man listed a number of names, but did not mention Imam Ali. Omar replied, "What do they have against [Imam Ali]? By God, he is the most qualified amongst them if they wished him to set them on the path of truth."[7]

They also knew that if Imam Ali was given his rightful place as the leader of the nation, he would have ample opportunity to show the truth and the rightful place of the Prophet's Progeny. As such, Imam Ali would institutionalize the rightful authority of the Household of the Prophet, putting an end to the Quraysh's utilization of political power for their own interests.

---

[6] Al-Mutazili, *Sharh Nahj Al-Balagha*, 1:186.
[7] Al-San'ani, *Al-Musannaf*, 10:357.

Even if the nation had forgotten the place of the Prophet's Household, they should not have forgotten the rightful place of the Quran and the tradition of the Prophet. Yet they still equated the precedence of the first two caliphs to the words of God and His Prophet.

In these circumstances, Imam Ali made his stance by accepting the first two conditions and rejecting the third. This led to Othman's accession to the caliphate, but Imam Ali had remained steadfast by his principles.

Imam Ali was still unable to publically denounce the perversity of the third condition as the groundwork was still not set. There were some amongst his supporters that had attempted to push him towards claiming his right by force. However, he knew that it would not be in the benefit of the faith nor was it the proper time to rise.

A companion of his by the name of Jundub once called him to claim his right by the sword. Imam Ali asked him, "Do you seek that one in ten people would give allegiance to me?" Jundub replied, "Yes, I do." To that, Imam Ali said, "But I do not seek that. By God, I do not seek even one in a hundred [to follow me]." When Jundub asked Imam Ali if he should call people to pledge allegiance to him, the Imam replied, "O' Jundub, this is not the time for it."[8]

This was the situation in Medina, where the companions of the Prophet had lived with Imam Ali and witnessed the quality of his character. We can only imagine what the situation would have been in the remainder of the caliphate's provinces.

---

[8] Al-Mutazili, *Sharh Nahj Al-Balagha*, 9:57.

## Othman's Character

Othman was different from his predecessor. For one, he was not as resolute and capable in the issues of government. More importantly, Othman was not prudent in handling the wealth of the public treasury. The signs of extravagance grew around him and his kin, as soon as he ascended to power.

Othman made the Umayyad clan the foundation of his government, despite their well-known history of opposition to the Prophet and his teachings. They were amongst the known hypocrites of the formative years of Islam. When they were given authority over the Muslims during Othman's caliphate, they used the treasury like their personal wealth. They treated the public as nothing more than their lowly subjects and servants. The Umayyads left no sanctity undefiled.

Both the public and the elite were disadvantaged by the Umayyads' rise in power and the policies the new caliphate enacted. Many of the chieftains that had benefitted under the rule of the first two caliphs were distraught to see that the lion's share of the spoils had been diverted toward the Umayyad clan. The public grew resentful of the ever increasing wealth gap in the kingdom due to the caliph's preferential policies. The religious leaders of the community were livid when they saw that Islam's sworn enemies had been made the governors of the nation.

With this, public sentiment toward Othman began to sour. With this, the ground was set and the winds of change began to blow.

## ALI'S OPPORTUNITY

With this, the opportunity arose for Imam Ali and his followers to further spread the message of the Prophet and his Household. It was Imam Ali who was the only party opposing Othman and his ilk before their accession to power. He had been deliberately distanced from the political system as his principled ideas did not suit the interests of the ruling class.

Imam Ali had the credentials that others lacked. He was the first male to enter Islam and was always at the side of the Prophet. Those who supported Imam Ali were the closest companions of the Prophet and had a great stature amongst the Muslims.

It was in these circumstances that Imam Ali and his followers saw their opportunity. They could freely voice their dissent. The religion was no longer in its formative and critical stage. It had spread across a large portion of the known world. It had emerged from the small city of Mecca and become a world religion.

There was no longer a need to fear being the cause of disunity amongst the Muslims. Disunity had already spread due to Othman's nepotism and incompetence. They no longer feared aggravating the situation, as it had already reached its lowest. They set out to spread their message. If people accepted it, the nation as a whole will see the benefits. And if people reject it, Imam Ali and his followers would have fulfilled their duty to call towards what is right.

We cannot list here all the historical accounts that support this conclusion. It is enough to realize that the public had begun to call Ali's name during the last days of Othman's rule, despite the fact that Imam Ali was the most lenient of opposition leaders toward Othman.

Yet it seems highly likely that Imam Ali and his followers had utilized the opportunity only to the extent possible and did not push their message to a degree that the people would not accept. The public was still not ready to be reminded of the message of Ali's divine appointment as the Prophet's successor. The caliphs' propaganda had made it impracticable to preach the virtues and rights of the Holy Household especially as the divinely appointed guardians of the faith and vicegerents of the Prophet. The most that Imam Ali and his followers were able to spread during that time were the virtues of the Progeny and their unmatched worthiness of leadership – regardless of the divine mandate.

Despite Othman's detested policies, the public still held a great deal of reverence for the first two caliphs.[9] Othman may have even served to solidify that reverence, as his reign was seen as a sharp contrast to theirs. Their reign was characterized by the expansion of the state and prosperity that was brought about by the spoils of war. His reign, however, was characterized by nepotism and corruption.

This is in addition to the fact that there was a broad opposition to Othman, many of whose leaders did not support Imam Ali or his claim to a divine mandate. After all, that would severely diminish their chances to grab hold of the throne.

---

[9] See, for example: Al-Kulayni, Al-Kafi, 8:58-63.

## OPPOSITION TO OTHMAN

Amongst the general public, opposition to Othman was driven by two outlooks. The majority amongst the opposition detested the conditions under Othman's reign and sincerely sought the betterment of their lives and the rest of society. They wanted a just and competent government that would look out for the interest of the public rather than the interests of the few.

There were also some amongst the opposition that saw this as an opportunity to further their own agendas. Some of the elites had lost many of the benefits that they gained under the first two caliphs, and thus they wished to regain those benefits through dissent. Others wished to use this opposition to gain such advantages and become part of the elite.

Neither of these groups had a clear plan to achieve their goals. They simply took the path of opposition in hopes that their interest would be served.

Imam Ali made earnest efforts to counsel Othman and reform his government. He knew that the public had turned against Othman and sought to avert sedition amongst the nation. When a delegation had come to him complaining of Othman's policies, Imam Ali went to Othman and said,

> ... *And I swear to you by God that you should not be the killed leader of this nation. It was said that a leader amongst this nation will be killed after which killing and fighting will become rampant until the Day of Judgment. He will confuse their matters and spread troubles over them.*

*As a result, they will not discern truth from falsity and will oscillate like waves and would be utterly misled.[10]*

Imam Ali had made strides in resolving the disputes that rose. However, Othman's incompetence, corruption amongst his courtiers, and the weakness of his character, all thwarted Imam Ali's efforts.

The situation continued to deteriorate leading to Othman's assassination. The staunch opposition against Othman had even prevented his family from burying his body. It wasn't until Imam Ali intervened on their behalf and that they were allowed to arrange a proper burial.[11]

## ALLEGIANCE TO IMAM ALI

The masses of the Muslims gravitated towards Imam Ali. They wanted to appoint him as their leader, as they knew very well of his character and principles. He was their hope for a competent and just nation that protected all of its citizens.

But Imam Ali knew his nation well. He refused to accept people's allegiances, as he knew that they would not be able to bear his justice. He said,

*Leave me and seek someone else. We are facing a matter with several options and many preferences. [You call for change that] hearts are not ready to bear and minds are unwilling to accept. Clouds are hovering overhead. The path has disguised itself. You should know that if I respond to you I would lead you as I know [I should lead]. I would not*

---

[10] Al-Radi, *Nahj Al-Balagha*, 2:69.
[11] Al-Mutazili, *Sharh Nahj Al-Balagha*, 2:158, 10:6.

*listen to the utterance of any speaker or the reproach of any admonisher. If you leave me then I am the same as you are. In fact, I may be the one who listens best and obeys whomever you make in charge of your affairs. I am better for you as a counselor than as chief.*[12]

Still, history tells us that the public refused his wishes. They were fed up with the corruption of previous rulers and longed for his justice. And so he obliged.

Allegiance was paid to Imam Ali. But that did not put an end to sedition. Less than five years passed before he was assassinated while he was praying in the Grand Mosque of Kufa.

In those five years, Imam Ali did not establish a stable government for the Household of the Prophet. The just government that he established did not last beyond his assassination. His son Imam Hassan was forced to make peace with Muawiya, who came to power and put an end to Imam Ali's reforms. All this is well recorded in the books of history.

At first sight, it might seem that Imam Ali's plans had failed. There was no lasting success. Rather, the nation was embroiled in civil war in the years of Imam Ali's tenure. Many Muslims lost their lives and the end result was Muawiya's accession to power and the creation of the Umayyad dynasty.

Yet Imam Ali knew from the beginning that the reform that the nation had sought when they first charged him with the caliphate was unachievable. He said it clearly when he re-

---

[12] Al-Radi, *Nahj Al-Balagha*, 1:181.

fused to accept allegiance at the outset, asserting that "We are facing a matter with several options and many preferences. [You call for change that] hearts are not ready to bear and minds are unwilling to accept."[13]

## IMAM ALI'S ACHIEVEMENTS

From this it seems clear that Ali's mission was not to bring about the change that the public wanted. It was evident to him that what they sought was practically unachievable. Rather, what had pushed him to take the seat of the caliphate was a promise that he had made to the Prophet. This is evident from his words,

> *Surely, by Him who split the grain [to grow] and created all living beings! If people had not come to me and supporters had not exhausted the argument – and if there had not been a pledge to God for the learned that they should not acquiesce in the gluttony of the oppressor and the hunger of the oppressed – I would have cast the reins [of the caliphate] over its shoulders [i.e. as to let it go]. I would have treated this last opportunity the way I treated the first. Then you would have seen that in my view this world of yours is no better than the sneezing of a goat.[14]*

From reading the accounts of history, we find that Imam Ali achieved at least two primary goals: clarifying religious truths and clarifying the rules of engagement.

---

[13] Al-Radi, *Nahj Al-Balagha*, 2:69.
[14] Al-Radi, *Nahj Al-Balagha*, 1:36-37.

## Clarifying Religious Truths

As we clarified previously, the Muslim nation had been put on a trajectory of fabrication and distortions of the faith. The true teachings of Islam would have been lost had the Household of the Prophet not been its prudent safeguards. Fabrications and distortions had been institutionalized for so many years.

But the opportunity had materialized for Imam Ali and his followers to utilize government institutions to clarify the true teachings of the faith. It was an opportunity to circulate, if only for a brief period, the true message of Islam. He made this clear when he said,

> *Oh God! You know that we did not seek power nor sought to acquire anything from the vanities of the world. We rather wanted to restore the signs of Your religion and to usher reform into Your cities so that the oppressed amongst Your creatures might be safe and Your forsaken commands might be established.*[15]

Imam Ali set out to propagate the proper teachings of Islam. He moved to Kufa, where he found a more receptive crowd. As his base of followers began to grow, he began to explain to them the truth of the God's divine mandate. He explained how the Prophet appointed him as the rightful successor and guardian of the message, and that this right would be passed down to the divinely guided Imams of the Prophet's Progeny.

He also explained that the 'unity' that the Prophet had valued and commanded the Muslims to abide by was not simp-

---

[15] Al-Radi, *Nahj Al-Balagha*, 2:13.

ly cohesion regardless of circumstance. Rather, the command for 'unity' meant that Muslims must be united in the protection of truth and justice. This truth and justice would only be achieved if people were united in support of God's chosen vicegerents – the Household of the Prophet.[16]

All this can be found in the records of history and in the words of Imam Ali – especially in *Nahj Al-Balagha*, an anthology of his sermons, letters, and short sayings.

Of course, Imam Ali's few years in government also served to solidify his following. He was in a position where people could see his actions and hear his words. They were reminded of his character and virtues. They remembered that he was the first man to believe in the message of the Prophet and was his greatest supporter. They remembered his valor in battle as he led them from the front lines during the civil wars that plagued his tenure. He was also the chief judge of the nation during those years, and so the nation saw the extent of his knowledge and justice. They saw his humility, modesty, and sincerity, even as he was the ruler of a vast nation. They saw his foretelling of hidden truths, all of which came to pass.

They saw that he was not an ordinary individual. They saw that he had a link to the divine, and that he was the rightful successor to the Prophet.

They were amazed by him. They grew attached to him. They loved him. They were devoted to him.

With that, the tree of Shia Islam that the Prophet planted in the hearts and minds of his most loyal companions – and

---

[16] See: Al-Hindi, *Kanz Al-Ummal*, 16:183-84.

which had almost withered away under the policies of the preceding caliphs – was again nurtured by the love of Imam Ali. Despite all the hardships and turmoil, he watered that tree and cared for it. Its roots developed, spread and dug deeper into the ground. Its branches would grow and extend towards the skies. By the time of the advent of Imam Hussain's revolution, the tree was ready to give its fruits.

Nonetheless, what remained as an obstacle in the path of Imam Ali and his message was the reverence that was held for the first two caliphs. This reverence was the cause of many amongst the public to deride the followers of Imam Ali and the Progeny and to transgress against them. The devotees of the Alid line were slaughtered, their wealth was looted, and the sanctity of their families was violated. Yet the devotion of the Shia never withered.

In summary, Imam Ali had successfully used those few years in power to spread the teachings of the Holy Household and solidify his following. He did so using clear signs and textual proofs. It was done against the context of the widely held belief that succession to the Prophet was not restricted to his Household, as well as the popularized reverence for the first two caliphs.

## Clarifying the Rules of Engagement

Othman's reign and subsequent assassination were primary causes of discord and disunity amongst the Muslims – a matter that led to a great deal of bloodshed. Imam Ali had predicted this on the day that allegiance was given to Oth-

man. He said to the members of the *Shura*,[17] who had selected Othman as caliph,

> *Hear my word and remember what I say. Perhaps you will*
> *soon see after today when swords will be drawn and pledges*
> *will be broken over this matter — so much so that some of*
> *you will become leaders of the people of misguidance and fol-*
> *lowers of the people of ignorance.*[18]

These mutinies that Imam Ali described did not come to be
until his tenure. Before that, the nation was unfamiliar with
civil war. As far as the public knew, the only wars that were
waged were against foreign powers such as the Sassanids
and the Byzantines. In those wars, the public did not have
much of a stake and the rulers were free to make and break
the rules of engagement as they pleased without oversight.

**Early Civil War**

Of course, the caliphate had waged war on Muslims before,
although government propaganda had masterfully painted it
as a war between states rather than a civil war.

Immediately after the passing of the Prophet, the caliphate
gained its control and solidified it through a number of
armed campaigns. Those campaigns were called the Wars of
Apostasy. The caliphate won, and as the victor it gained the
license of writing history in their favor. It masterfully paint-

---

[17] The Shura, or council, refers to a delegation of six men that Omar appointed and assigned them with the task of choosing the next caliph.
The men were: Ali ibn Abu Talib, Abd al-Rahman ibn Awf, Saad ibn
Abu Waqqas, Othman ibn Affan, Zubayr ibn Al-Awwam, and Talhah
ibn Ubaydullah. –Eds.

[18] Al-Mutazili, *Sharh Nahj Al-Balagha*, 1:195.

ed this armed struggle as a rightful clash against treason and apostasy.

The truth was far more complex. There were some who did reject the faith and became apostates after the death of the Prophet. But that was by no means the only reason behind these wars. In fact, the chief purpose for the wars was to solidify the authority of the newly founded caliphate.

The tribe of Kindah was one tribe that was not fought for the purpose of apostasy. It is not within the scope of this book to relate the historical account of these battles, as it is quite lengthy and detailed. Nonetheless, we will mention a few details of the revolt of Kindah. When the first caliph assumed political authority over the Muslim nation, he began to collect religious dues and taxes from the tribes that had accepted Islam. Kindah was one of the tribes that refused to pay these taxes to Abu Bakr, asserting that he had no authority over them. One would say,

> We obeyed the Messenger of God when he was alive, and if a man of his household were to rise, we would obey as well. As for [Abu Bakr], we shall not. By God, he has no right over us to give him obedience or allegiance.

Another would tell Abu Bakr's deputy,

> By God, you only usurped it away from its rightful holders because of your envy. I cannot accept in my heart that the Messenger of God left this world without appointing for the people a guide to follow. So leave us, as you are calling for something that will not be accepted.

Yet another would declare,

*Remove [Abu Bakr's deputy] from amongst you! His man
is not suited for succession and he does not deserve it in any
respect. The Muhajiroon and the Ansar[19] are not better
judges of [the needs of this nation] than its Prophet Muhammad.[20]*

This is all to clarify that, despite having fought Muslims before, the public did not realize that such battles took place.
They were ignorant of when such battles are warranted and
how they should be conducted. Imam Ali would clarify all
this through his leadership.

**Imam Ali's Tradition**

The embroilment of Imam Ali's government in successive
civil wars was a means for him to clarify the rules of war
amongst Muslims. Decades later, Abu Hanifa would say,

*Imam Ali did not fight anyone except that the truth was on
his side. If it wasn't for Imam Ali's tradition on treating
[his enemies], no one would know the [proper rules of en-
gagement] amongst Muslims.[21]*

Through his tradition, Imam Ali clarified that although the
aggressor in such a civil war may face death, there can be no
enslavement of Muslim prisoners of war. Whatever wealth

---

[19] The *Ansar* is a term used in Islam in reference to the inhabitants of
the city of Medina at the time of the Prophet's migration to the city.
They aided the Prophet and allowed him to establish his capital in their
city, and so they came to be known as the *Ansar* – literally, supporters –
of the Prophet. The term is usually used to distinguish them from the
*Muhajiroon* – literally, migrants – who came from Mecca along with the
Prophet and lived alongside their *Ansar* brethren in Medina. The two
groups are not inclusive of all Muslims – many converted to Islam and
continued to live outside the boundaries of these two cities. –Eds.
[20] Ibn A'tham, *Al-Futuh*, 1:49-57.
[21] Ibn Abu Jurada, *Bughyat Al-Talab*, 1:291.

was not used in battle would not be subject to plundering as part of the war spoils.[22] Some even suggest that wealth that was used in the waging of war would not be subject to plundering.[23]

The Muslims had not made this distinction between wars waged amongst Muslims and wars that were waged against disbelievers. And when Imam Ali won the first civil war during his tenure at the Battle of the Camel, he was urged by his camp to take the prisoners of war as slaves. Yet Imam Ali understood that this would have been a grave crime. He wittingly convinced his camp with a jesting statement that allowed them to see what a grave mistake it would be, "Then set a lottery for Aisha so that I can give her to the winner."[24] The irony being that everyone knew Aisha, as the widow of their Prophet and the Mother of the Believers[25] could not be taken into slavery as any other prisoner of war. Of course, Imam Ali's wit was not simply employed to protect the widow of the Prophet but to protect the rights of all the Muslims.

Imam Ali took the high road when dealing with his opponents. He could have easily enslaved them and plundered their riches as a form of vengeance for their crimes. The people did not know the error of this. It would certainly have made him more popular amongst his army, which was thirsty for the spoils of war. In fact, when people saw that there would be no spoils from these civil wars, the ranks of

---

[22] Al-Mutazili, *Sharh Nahj Al-Balagha*, 1:250.

[23] Al-Najafi, *Jawahir Al-Kalaam*, 21:339-41.

[24] Ibn Abu Jurada, *Bughyat Al-Talab*, 1:291.

[25] An honorary title given to the wives of Prophet Muhammad in the Quran. See: The Holy Quran, 33:6. –Eds.

his army began to dwindle. But Imam Ali could not turn a blind eye to what was right. He was committed to abiding by God's commands and implementing His will.

Any brief glimpse into the dynasties that followed Imam Ali's tenure would show that these rules of engagement were not upheld or respected. The caliphs of the Umayyad and Abbasid dynasties especially contradicted these teachings. But as we discussed earlier, Imam Ali's goal was not to set a precedent that would be followed by future caliphs – he knew that the power hungry chieftains that would seize the throne would never live by these standards. Rather, Imam Ali established a standard that succeeding generations could use to evaluate their rulers and hold them accountable for their actions.

# UMAYYAD PLOYS

Imam Ali did not remain long as the head of the Muslim state. As soon as he was ushered into power by a popular uprising against predecessor, sedition and civil war began to brew. Imam Ali did not complete five years in the position of political authority before he was assassinated. His son, Imam Hassan, rose to continue the legacy of his father. However, he too was faced with great opposition and ultimately signed his bitter accord with Muawiya. The legacies that Imam Ali and Imam Hassan left behind will be discussed in the coming chapters.

And so Muawiya seized the caliphate and set to establish the lasting rule of the Umayyad dynasty. The nation's morale sunk to a new low. Muawiya continued to utilize the propaganda tools employed in the past to shape and shift the nation's religion and culture to best suit Umayyad interests. The Umayyad clan had come to control the nation's fate and faith.

## ELIMINATING THE ALID LINE

At first, Muawiya seemed content with his policies of extortion and bribery, thinking that it would be enough to eliminate the Alid line. He thought that whoever had followed Imam Ali in the past did so because Imam Ali wielded political authority and controlled the treasury. He did not realize that Imam Ali's supporters were not actually devoted to him because of any material benefits.

He thought that after Imam Ali's assassination and Imam Hassan's peace accord, the Household of the Prophet would be forgotten.

He was surprised to find that Imam Ali had taken his place in the hearts and minds of many in the nation, and continued to have that influence even after his assassination. Muawiya would exclaim to Imam Ali's followers, "By God! Your loyalty to him after his death is more astounding than your love for him when he was alive."[1]

Imam Ali's message had a deep theological dimension, which stood as a hurdle to Muawiya's ploys. The teachings of the Alids became a rallying cry for a staunch opposition against Muawiya.

### Clear Proofs

In his short tenure as caliph of the Muslim nation, Imam Ali spread the idea of the primacy of the Household of the Prophet through a number of intellectual and textual proofs.

---

[1] Al-Andalusi, *Al-'Iqd Al-Fareed*, 2:83.

One of the most important proofs that Imam Ali and his followers publicized was the Tradition of the House – where the Prophet gathered his family and clan and called them to believe in the message of God. With his declaration of the Prophecy, the Messenger of God asked everyone present if any of them would support him and be his vizier and vicegerent. No one answered the call but the young Ali ibn Abu Talib, who became the first male to believe in the Prophet's call.[2]

Another one of these important proofs was the Tradition of Ghadeer. After his Farewell Pilgrimage, the Prophet gathered all the Muslims that had joined him at a place called Ghadeer Khum. In the heat of the desert, he ascended a makeshift pulpit built of large stones, saddles and sheets of cloth, and addressed the thousands in his midst. By divine command, he informed the believers of his nearing death. As the Muslims wept over the news, he told them that there was a key to success and guidance after him – holding on to both the Book of God and the Prophet's Household. The Prophet sealed the address with the declaration of succession after his demise. "Whomever I am his master, Ali is his master." Thousands of Muslims witnessed the Prophet's declaration that Imam Ali was the leader, guide, and protector of the nation after him.[3]

And there are many other similar traditions.

Imam Ali did not do this alone. He was supported by a loyal corps of supporters. They were at his side and spread his message during the reign of Othman. They continued by his

---

[2] Al-Tabari, *Tareekh Al-Tabari*, 2:63-64.
[3] Al-Shaybani, *Musnad Ahamd*, 3:370.

side during his tenure and the great turmoil of the civil wars that ensued.

In fact, this corps gained momentum and grew beyond its small size. It was no longer a movement limited to a close group of Imam Ali's companions. Rather, it began to expand and include many who were disillusioned with the fact that the Umayyad clan was gaining power and preference throughout the nation.

## Emotion and Experience

Imam Ali's movement was not simply an intellectual one based on evidence and proof. Rather, it involved a significant emotional dimension. Imam Ali and his family had the closest conceivable connection to the Prophet, granting them a great deal of love and reverence in the hearts of believers. Furthermore, the experience that the people had with Umayyad authority only served to remind them of the justice and forbearance of the Prophet and the Holy Household.

In addition, the failure of the ideology that the caliphate was based upon became evident. It was this philosophy that led to the empowerment of the Umayyad clan during Othman's reign and later led to the establishment of the Umayyad dynasty – despite the fact that they were Islam's greatest enemies and had openly disregarded the sanctity of Muslim life and property.

Usurping the position of successorship after the Prophet was the primary cause for the distortion, corruption, and turmoil the Muslim nation faced. The chieftains that first ascended to the caliphate were not designated by God and

His Prophet, nor were they restricted by a set of standards and qualifications to ensure just and rightful rule. Thus, a person like Muawiya was able to seize the title of 'Successor to the Prophet' through force and trickery.

This was exactly what Lady Fatima predicted in the months following the Prophet's death, when she proclaimed,

> [The tree] has been fertilized, so wait until it gives its fruit! You will fill your cauldrons with newly spilt blood and deadly poison. On that day 'the falsifiers will fail'[4] and the wretched will realize the results of what their predecessors established. There, you must let yourselves be comforted away from this world and muster fortitude in the face of sedition. Give tidings to a piercing sword, the tyranny of a repressive aggressor, enveloping pandemonium, and despotism on the side of oppressors that will leave your livelihoods meager and your band an [easy] harvest.[5]

Imam Ali strengthened people's relationship to the tenets and principles of Shia Islam through the intellectual and emotional dimensions discussed. This all would have led to the spread of the Shia faith across the nation, had trickery and deception not been used to deviate the people away from this path.

## MUAWIYA'S DECEPTION

Realizing all this, Muawiya set out to hinder the growth of the Shia school of thought. He used force, trickery, and deception to achieve this end.

---

[4] The Holy Quran, 45:27.
[5] Ibn Tayfour, *Balaghat Al-Nisa*, 19-20.

He began with the systematic persecution of the Shia and used the Umayyad propaganda machine to paint them in the most negative light. He cut them off from the public treasury. He killed them and mutilated their bodies. He imprisoned many and exiled many more. He destroyed the homes of any family that was suspect of leaning toward Imam Ali's path. The Umayyads became so bent on devastating the followers of Imam Ali that historians say, "Whenever they heard of a newborn named Ali they would kill him."[6]

Still, they were unable to destroy the Shia. They were a people of fortitude and perseverance. Instead, the persecution they faced served the Shia in the long run. Persecution only invigorates the call of truth. Persecution gave the Shia a renewed strength and pride in their faith. People became more compassionate and sympathetic to their cause.

*Fabrication and Misinformation*

Moreover, the Umayyad clan sought to stifle the spread of true prophetic traditions once more. But Muawiya was not content with simply preventing the spread of these traditions. Instead, he used the bully pulpit to spread whatever lies and fabrications strengthened his rule.

Firstly, Muawiya criminalized the narration of any of the virtues of the Holy Household or any other tradition that would serve their school of thought. He also criminalized the narration of anything that derogates the opponents of the Holy Household.

Secondly, he set in motion a propaganda campaign that aimed to disparage and belittle the Holy Household, espe-

---

[6] Ibn Asakir, *Tareekh Dimashq*, 41:481.

cially Imam Ali. This resulted in numerous fabrications. However, it seems that many of the individuals that recorded books of tradition opted to disregard these in their books. Not only were such blatant lies clearly fabricated by a government that harbored such hatred and envy for the Prophet's family, but it was also a point of weakness and an easy target for anyone who wished to show the feebleness of the prevalent ideology. These lies became an embarrassment for those ascribing to the prevalent ideology espoused by the state.

Thus, these attempts to derogate and belittle the Prophet's family were unsuccessful. They did see little success in areas like the Levant, where the Umayyads had complete control of the narrative and where there was no considerable opposition. But by and large, this second method was essentially a failure.

Thirdly, the Umayyad propaganda machine would fabricate lies praising a specific group of companions that held an animus toward the Holy Household, especially the early caliphs. This was the forte of a group of charlatans who feigned piety and fabricated lies, in order to gain influence in the Umayyad courts along with grand gifts of wealth and estates from the public treasury. And although the falsity of such lies was evident to many,[7] they were not as easily rejected and were still recorded by many books of narration.

As we mentioned earlier, such fabrications began from the time of the early caliphs. This created a great deal of reverence for those early caliphs in the hearts of the masses. It

---

[7] See, for example: Al-Fayrouzabadi, *Sifr Al-Sa'ada*, 143.

led to a justification of all their misdeeds and a blind trust in their 'rightly guided' status. In addition, people were very receptive to those traditions because of the great wealth that the early caliphs' conquest campaigns brought to many within the territories of the state.

Muawiya realized that this was a strong tool to use for stifling the spread of the school of the Holy Household. It is one thing to combat a religious ideology with material means. It is another thing – and usually more effective – to combat a religious ideology with an alternative ideology. With one generation after the other, people began to grow more attached and fanatical in their ideologies. These fabrications especially had two primary negative impacts on the Muslim nation.

First, it stood as a counterpoint to the traditions that stressed the right and primacy of the Holy Household. Muawiya always tried to deride Imam Ali because of his stance against the early caliphs. These fabrications served to further imbed reverence for those caliphs and other companions that stood against the Household of the Prophet. They provided an alternate to the idea of Imam Ali's divine appointment by creating an unabashed reverence for the early caliphs.

Second, they gave the Umayyads a great deal of power to distort the message of the Prophet. All Muslims agree, with the exception of a few outliers, that there must be a leader who unifies the Muslim nation. The Shia believe that such a leader must be divinely appointed. Others adopted the state endorsed idea that this leadership is legitimate even if it is acquired and effectuated by the edge of the sword. The lies and fabrications propagated by the Umayyad clan served to strengthen this second point of view, weakening the popularity of the view held by followers of the Holy Household.

It naturally follows that when the public gives such high regard to whomever forcefully seizes the throne, anyone who holds that seat wields the power to distort the faith by the dictates of his interests. In addition, the precedent of the early caliphs was to equate political authority with religious authority, giving greater credence to this school of thought. Thus, this allowed the Umayyads to pose an even greater danger, not only to Muslims as persons, but also to Islam as a message and a faith.

## The Fallout

What aggravated the situation further was that Muawiya had been setting the stage for his son Yazid to become heir to the throne. He sought to create a dynasty for his son and grandchildren. Islam and its dominion became a mere tool to prop up such a dynasty.

The Umayyads were well known as sworn enemies of Islam during the Prophet's lifetime. They only embraced the faith because they saw it as their only means to survival. They had participated in the battles against the Prophet, where many of their kin were killed. Their staunch opposition and armed hostility to the message of Islam had cost them the loss of family members and social status. They sought revenge for the former and a restoration for the latter.

It was evident to all their contemporaries that they had only accepted Islam through lip service. It had changed nothing about them. They abided by none of its values. They transgressed against every sanctity and principle to reach their goals and advance their tribal interests.

This reality is heartrending to any Muslim. But it should not come as a surprise that history took this turn after the death of the Prophet. It is the natural conclusion for usurpation of the rights of the Prophet's divinely chosen successors. With each passing generation where fabrications were allowed to continue and the people stood by their deviant and repressive regime, the situation only became worse. Without the proper guide, people begin to lose their way and neglect the principles of their faith.

# A NECESSARY TRAGEDY

Muawiya achieved his goal – he established a dynasty for his kin based on tribal alliances and tendencies. He used religion as a means to achieve his desired ends, even if it meant relying on fabrication and distortion.

If the nation had continued in this trajectory, it would have been able to completely reverse Imam Ali's achievements. It would have undone all that the Household of the Prophet had been able to accomplish in terms of educating the nation and spreading the true message of Islam.

Muawiya was successful in building a strong and stable state. He used tactics of terror and extortion to achieve this goal. He created a vast propaganda machine in order to spread lies and fabrications. He agitated and utilized bigotry and tribal tendencies for these purposes.

The chieftains throughout the nation abandoned the standards and principles that the Prophet had taught. They raced to please the tyrants and gain their favor. The public became acclimated to this condition. This became – at least to the perception of the general public – the reality of governance and the religion which the state claimed to represent.

Muawiya clarified this in his will to his son Yazid, where he said,

> *My son, I have sufficed you many journeys. I prepared matters for you. I humiliated enemies for you. I made the necks of the Arabs subservient to you...*[1]

## AGONY IN THE FACE OF DEVIANCE

Nonetheless, there was a group of individuals who remained cognizant of the true principles of the faith, or at least feigned to be so. They were agonizing, or bluffing agony, over the tragedy that had befallen the religion of the Grand Prophet. How could they not when a state had come about that claimed to represent the religion while relentlessly undermining its cause, deviating from its teachings, and oppressing its followers.

Yet none seemed to realize or care about the distortions that the regime had affected in their religion. That is why their vision was limited to desiring a change of regime and nothing more. Even if they knew where political leadership should rightfully lie, their conception of the problem was limited to the political dimension at stake.

This sort of individuals can be divided into two types. There were those who saw this mission as a practical undertaking that they must endeavor to achieve. Some used trickery and deception as a tool to reach this end, with hopes of attaining power and affluence after any kind of political change. Others were well intentioned, reacting to the apparent corruption of the state. Among this second subgroup were the loy-

---

[1] Al-Tabari, *Tareekh Al-Tabari*, 4:238.

al devotees of the Progeny of the Prophet – the ones who had been pressing Imam Hussain to revolt much like they had pressed his brother Imam Hassan before. They saw the death of Muawiya as an opportunity that could not be foregone.

The second type of individuals saw political change as impracticable, as they did not think they had enough support and resources to effectuate any real change. They were disheartened after witnessing the perceived failure of Imam Ali's efforts in reforming the Muslim nation. They weighed the costs and benefits of any revolution, and saw that the costs dwarfed any perceivable benefit.

They knew that they could not find a better leader than Imam Ali – with his knowledge of the faith, dedication to the mission, principled nature, unshakable devotion, courage in confrontation, and status among the Muslims. No one could hold more legitimacy than Imam Ali, especially after the Muslim community gave him allegiance.

Neither could they find supporters like those who had aided Imam Ali. He had garnered the allegiance of the vast majority of Muslims, including a great number of companions of the Holy Prophet. His closest companions were amongst the noblest of the Muslim nation, and they made great sacrifices in his aid.

And neither could there be a time and era better than the era of Imam Ali. There were still many who had seen the Prophet and heard his words. Imam Ali himself was first and foremost amongst the Prophet's companions. The further time stretched away from the era of the Prophet, the more obscure his teachings became to the public. This is especially true given the deviance of the state and its constant attempts to distort the teachings of Islam.

Indeed, history has not recorded any period in Islam, where a reform movement was able to take hold for so long a period and with such an effect, much like the era of Imam Ali.

Those who read into the history of the Muslim nation will clearly see that the military collapse of Imam Ali's movement was only due to his firm stance of principle. His enemies were able to use that against him in their conniving ploys.

For these reasons, the second group mentioned above sought to minimize the losses and refrain from any active attempts at changing the Umayyad regime. And this may be the reasoning behind many of the voices that counseled Hussain to refrain from crossing Yazid, including those of Abdullah ibn Jaafar and Muhammad ibn Al-Hanafiyya.

Moreover, the further the state delves into its corruption and spills the blood of innocents, the more it will be accustomed to crossing the line. This is more so when the innocent blood spilled is that of the grandson of the Prophet, his family, and his companions.

Add to this two additional factors that had influence on people: cowardice in the face of a powerful enemy, and fear of dividing the Muslim nation which tyrannical powers had for so long grasped as justification.

## ASSESSING THE CIRCUMSTANCES

The Progeny was fully aware that correcting the deviance of the state was impractical in the short term. As we discussed earlier, Imam Ali knew that such a task was not achievable in the brief period of his tenure. He knew that his reform movement would inevitably be overcome by the Umayyad forces that took hold after his assassination. His goal was not a military success or the establishment of a state governed by the Progeny. Rather, his goal was to showcase the true teachings of the Quran and embody the principles of the Prophet during his tenure. He wanted to draw a clear example of a righteous statesman, so that the public can see the villainous and deviant nature of the others by comparison. He aimed to create a clear unequivocal distinction between the true teachings of the Prophet and the fabrications that had been popularized by the chieftains before and after him. In this, he was successful.

And through his stance, he was able to raise a group of loyal supporters who understood his cause and supported it wholeheartedly.

Yet Imam Ali's achievements were in danger of being reverted due to Muawiya's deliberate actions – most importantly the coronation of his son Yazid as heir.

This was especially dangerous for a number of intrinsic factors. Yazid's contemptible nature was evident to all. He was a shameless miscreant, blatantly ridiculing the religion he would claim to represent and acting in complete contradiction to its teachings. Furthermore, Muawiya's selection of Yazid as successor threatened to establish a dangerous precedent. Effectively, Muawiya was looking to establish a dynasty for his heirs. He wished to eliminate the qualifications for holding public office and replace them with a hereditary right. He wished to prove that he held title to the lives of all Muslims and could pass it on to his heirs as he pleased.

A number of extrinsic factors aggravated the situation. The Umayyad state had become a powerful force, clenching tightly to the reins of power. Thus, correcting the path of the government was a near impossible task. In addition, the nation was struck with a severe bout of lethargy. It grew more and more heedless of the true teachings of the Prophet and inherently allowed its deviant rulers to continue in distorting the tenets of faith and the realities of history.

By the end of Muawiya's reign, the Muslim nation had reached an unsurpassed low – it was in dire need of a stance to be made. If the leaders of the Muslim nation – first and foremost, Imam Hussain himself – were to give allegiance to Yazid, there would be no stopping the nation's descent into the dark abyss Muawiya had created.

## Taqiyya

All this was exacerbated by the fact that the Muslim nation had not yet comprehended the concept of *taqiyya*.[2] They did not realize that they could comply with the oath of allegiance and remain silent in the face of deviance because of compulsion and duress – and that this would not give legitimacy to the state.

---

[2] *Taqiyya* – from the Arabic root *waqa*, meaning 'protected' – is a religious tenet that allows dissimulation for the purpose of preserving life, limb, and property. –Eds.

This was especially the case after a few notable companions, the likes of Hijr ibn Adi,[3] had decided not to act according to *taqiyya*, but stand in the face of tyranny and deviance. For their stance, they paid the ultimate price – their blood.[4]

Given the fact that the idea of *taqiyya* was not yet fully understood, Imam Hussain's circumstances did not allow him to effectively practice it and set its example for the people during his time. At that time, allegiance from him would be misunderstood to convey full legitimacy to a deviant such as Yazid.

It was not until after the tragedy of Karbala that the Imams would be able to spread an understanding and set examples for the practice of *taqiyya* through their actions. There are many examples that we can give in this regard, but we will suffice with one for brevity's sake.

Historians recount that, after the revolt in Hijaz,[5] the Umayyad commander Muslim ibn Uqba demanded the allegiance of the people of Medina. But a normal oath of allegiance

---

[3] Hijr ibn Adi Al-Kindi, a close companion of the Prophet and a follower of Ali ibn Abu Talib. He was known as an austere worshiper. He was killed by Muawiya after the assassination of Imam Ali. –Eds.

[4] The determination of these select few to make their stance and not act in accordance with *taqiyya* may be attributed to the fact that the true tenets of Islam that they had adopted were not clear to the rest of the Muslim nation. Thus, acting in accordance to *taqiyya* may have resulted in the truth being lost to the public and that would have been a greater harm to Islam – warranting a great sacrifice to repel such a great harm. Their stances were thus similar to the stance of Imam Hussain. This is in addition to the probability that their stances were made by the will and command of the Commander of the Faithful. But all this requires a lengthy discussion that lies outside the scope of this book. –Author

[5] The people of Hijaz revolted soon after the massacre at Karbala. They were bloodily put down in the battle of Harra. The events of this revolt are discussed further in the next chapter. –Eds.

was not enough – he sought to humiliate them by accepting nothing less than the concession that they are slaves and chattel of Yazid. Whoever did not concede was beheaded.

In the tumult of this scene, Imam Ali ibn Hussain – the man who had seen his family and friends massacred by Yazid's army not too long ago – came to Muslim ibn Uqba and said, "How does Yazid want me give you my oath of allegiance?" Muslim, in a voice of feigned reverence, said "That you are a brother and a cousin." Imam Ali ibn Hussain replied, "Yet if you wished, I would pledge allegiance as a slave and chattel." "I would not burden you by this," a flustered Muslim sputtered.[6]

Imam Ali ibn Hussain was especially in a position to spread an understanding of *taqiyya* through his actions. It was clear that his allegiance was not an admittance of legitimacy to the Umayyad caliphate. No one would even think that he would be giving any legitimacy to the government that had just slaughtered his father, uncles, brothers, cousins and companions. Rather, it was evident that his allegiance to the state was meant to avoid further bloodshed with the purpose of safeguarding the principles of the faith and its people. Through this he planted in the believers' awareness the priority of safeguarding the sanctity of life and the preservation of the principles of faith.

Such a ceremonial oath of allegiance – one that is given under duress – is by no means a show of loyalty or a grant of legitimacy. Partaking in such lip service in order to protect one's life and family is more desirable than to be killed at

---

[6] Al-Yaqoubi, Tareekh Al-Yaqoubi, 2:250-51.

the whims of tyrants. Unless such a death contributes to the long-term strategy of preserving the faith and its tenets, it is far better to survive and serve those principles. This was the understanding that Imams drove through their actions and examples.

## The Kharijites

Adding to the complexity of the situation, the only force that had risen against Umayyad rule before the tragedy of Karbala had been the Kharijites.[7]

They, however, did not hold any respect within Muslim society. It was abundantly clear that they based their call on an erroneous ideology that stood squarely against Imam Ali, a man whose righteousness they could not succeed in tainting. Moreover, they were an extreme and unruly bunch that did not respect the sanctity of Muslims' blood and wealth. All this created much antagonism for them amongst the general public.

The state knew this well. The Umayyads used the Kharijites' infamy against them and employed its propaganda machine to ostracize them in the eyes of the public. It is also interesting to see that, in the heat of the moment, Umayyad officials and propagandists had tried to paint Imam Hussain

---

[7] The Kharijites were a group of Muslims who believed that both Ali ibn Abu Talib and Muawiya should be removed because they went against established tradition when they appointed arbiters to decide their dispute after the Battle of Siffin. The Kharijites amassed an army and prepared to attack Ali ibn Abu Talib. Although Ali ibn Abu Talib was victorious against the Kharijite army in the Battle of Nahrawan, the remnants of the Kharijites would continue to cause trouble and would ultimately succeed in assassinating Ali ibn Abu Talib. –Eds.

and his supporters as Kharijites as well – a failed effort to defame the heroes of Karbala.

Therefore, the revolt of the Kharijites against Umayyad power did nothing to delegitimize the tyrannical state. Especially after so many respected Muslim leaders had given allegiance, willingly or under duress.

## The Shia

Other than the Kharijites, no one held the banner of opposition to the Umayyad state but the Shia. The Shia were amongst the most respectable Muslims in the nation. They were known for piety, knowledge, and honesty. In fact, all Muslims take the word of first century Shia narrators,[8] despite knowing that they ascribe to a different school of thought. A prominent scholar by the name of Sufyan Al-Thawri even said, "Have you seen the best of people to be anything but Shia?"[9]

This is despite the fact that the Shia held an ideology that was in direct contrast to what most of the Muslim public ascribed to. They refused to accept the legitimacy of the early caliphs and insisted that the rightful successors of the Prophet were his family and progeny. The Shia criticized the policies of the caliphs despite the great reverence bordering sanctification that the majority of Muslims had for them.

This was an intractable obstacle that faced the Shia in propagating their school of thought. And if Imam Hussain had given allegiance to Yazid, it would only have served to fur-

---

[8] In Islamic history, a narrator was an individual who memorized and relayed the speech, actions, and silent affirmations of the Prophet Muhammad and his family. –Eds.

[9] Al-Asfahani, *Maqatil Al-Talibiyyin*, 195.

ther dilute their position. Thus, the Shia had to face the greatest degrees of persecution at the hand of the state. This undoubtedly stifled the growth of their ideology.

## Trajectory of Distortion

If a state continues on this trajectory of distortion, it will become the status quo. The true teachings of the faith would soon be forgotten. The state that claimed to represent the faith will be, in the minds of many, the only representation of God's will.

Even if the powers change due to some external circumstances, the nation will continue to see whoever wields authority as the legitimate representative of the faith. The religion would continue in the trajectory of distortion that the state set it on. Successive regimes would continue to use religion as a tool to pursue their own ends.

Correcting this trajectory is no easy task. In the short term it is simply impossible. But standing silently as the nation heads down this road, especially in these dire circumstances, would be unacceptable. It would affirmatively allow the corrupt regimes to achieve their goals of distorting the faith in pursuit of their special interests.

The Umayyad regime was systematic in its attempts to alter the faith. It did not try to radically change the teachings of the Prophet overnight. Rather, it pursued a gradual approach. It would start at something minor and wait until the public gets acclimated to the change. Succeeding on one issue, it would then incrementally move to greater distortions that would play into their greater interests.

In this, they found a very useful precedent in the early caliphs who had practiced dominion over religious matters. With those early caliphs so revered in the minds of the public, their precedent could not be overturned. In addition, they utilized the miscreant orators and supposed narrators to fabricate texts that enshrine the caliphate as the ultimate authority on religious affairs.

The state was also systematic in weakening its opposition. It consistently harassed the leaders of the opposition. It blackmailed and extorted many to join its ranks. Increasingly, the state targeted opposition leaders which resulted in many gruesome massacres. All this diluted the ability of the opposition to stand in the face of the state and spread any message that did not suit state interests.

*Implications*

This produced two significant effects.

Firstly, people began to grow familiar with the state's brand of faith. They lost sight of the true tenets of their religion. Religion became less relevant to the lives of ordinary individuals. It became stale and ineffective. It became a mere set of rituals taken up every now and then to feed some sense of guilt.

This was exactly what Muawiya aimed to achieve. He used the tactics of extortion, bribery, tribalism, and distortion to achieve that end. He sought to taint the faith with the bloody crimes of the state. In that, people would begin to shy away from faith and see it as a tool for a tyrannical regime, doing with it as it wills. People began to search for every means to escape such an ideology. They gradually lost faith in the message.

This is exactly what happened to previous messages. The reader surely knows of the Dark Ages and how the image of religion was tarnished. Some of this was an effect of oppressive regimes' misuse of the religion in pursuit of their own special interests. Also playing a role was the corruption in religious establishments that worked hand-in-hand with the state to subdue and enslave nations.

Secondly, fabrications and distortions transformed religion into mythology. They imbedded contradictions that defied morality and reason. A rational individual was then left to a choice – either reject religion in its entirety, adopt it as a cultural phenomenon rather than out of true faith, or accept it blindly out of zeal and narrow-mindedness.

This is how history took its course when fabrications and distortions took hold of divine messages prior to Islam. In fact, it is true for much of Islamic heritage which lies defaced because of state meddling in and exploitation of religion. These blatant fabrications and distortions are now used by the enemies of Islam – rather, the enemies of faith as a whole – as a point of attack and ridicule. They are oblivious to the fact – or may at least pretend to be – that divine messages are innocent of such lies.

## QUAGMIRE

There was only one way to divert the nation away from this catastrophic trajectory. The state had entered a quagmire that would expose its true colors and leave it without justification in the eyes of the public. It would take its corruption one step further and too far, committing a heinous crime that provoked the Muslim nation as a whole. There had to be a tragedy that would shake the nation to its core and remind it of the true principles of its faith for centuries that followed.

Only then would the state lose its ability to control the nation's faith and fate – its ability to distort and indoctrinate. The public would no longer see itself as subjects and followers of the state. Rather, it would come to truly know its subjugation and oppression at the hands of the regime.

The opportunity for this to come to fruition came after the death of Muawiya. With the accession of Yazid, the Umayyad state hit a new low. Yazid possessed no qualification for governance and no quality for leadership. The nation wanted nothing to do with a man like him. Thus, the opportunity arose to reject any legitimacy for the state and remind the public of Umayyad crimes.

Yazid was a reckless brute. He did not care for wisdom and prudence. He got what he desired without calculating options or weighing repercussions – a temperament that was very different from his father's.

There was a select group of individuals who realized all this and were confident that change had become imminent. They put their trust in a leader – Imam Hussain – who they wholeheartedly believed was immaculate. They promised him their aid, even if it meant sacrificing their own souls for the greater cause.

The tragedy at Karbala – with its religious and emotional dimensions and within the scope of a divine plan discussed earlier – was the straw that broke the camel's back. Of course, it was no straw at all. It was the mountain of guilt and sorrow that would finally bring the nation back to its conscience.

What other crime could fulfill such a necessary role? The thoughtful amongst the Umayyad brass knew well what the massacre would mean. Waleed ibn Utba, Yazid's governor over Medina, articulated it when he sent a letter to Ubaydullah ibn Ziyad urging,

> *Hussain ibn Ali has headed to Iraq. He is the son of Fatima. Fatima is the daughter of the Messenger of God. So be wary and do not let any harm come to him. You would only be agitating [a fire] against yourself and your people [that cannot be smothered]. It will never be forgotten by the elite or by the masses for the remainder of eternity.*[10]

This all was foreshadowed by Imam Hussain in his conversation with his half-brother Muhammad ibn Al-Hanafiyya. Imam Hussain would tell his brother,

> *The Messenger of God came to me [i.e. in a vision] after I left you. He said to me, 'O Hussain. Set out [on your journey], for God has surely willed to see you as a martyr.'*

His brother Muhammad cried, "Surely, we belong to God and to Him we will return. But what is the meaning of taking the women with you if you are heading in such a state?"

---

[10] Al-Majlisi, *Bihar Al-Anwar*, 44:368.

Imam Hussain replied, "[The Prophet] had said to me, 'God has surely willed to see them as captives.'"[11]

In any case, this tragedy would be the culmination of what Imam Ali had started. To set the groundwork, Imam Hassan had made many sacrifices. He remained patient during the bitter accord with Muawiya, who would go on to violate only to be exposed for his true character. Imam Hassan endured being the target of lies and defamation even from within his own camp and still remained firm to his principle. Imam Hussain's tragedy would be the pinnacle, the climactic occasion that would expose truth from falsehood and save Islam from demise under the Umayyads.

## AUDACITY AND DIVISION

One of the repercussions of this tragedy, as discussed earlier, was an increased audacity on the part of the Umayyad state. After having massacred the family of the Prophet, the Umayyad army would have no quarrel with shedding more blood, no matter how sacred. Imam Hussain predicted this, as did others.

This would have been most dangerous if the state continued to hold legitimacy in the eyes of the public. That would have been the case had Imam Hussain complied with Yazid's demands and given allegiance. The state would then have both the audacity and the perceived legitimacy to pursue its interests by any means necessary. It would not be blamed for the shedding of blood and distorting faith. With that, the true message of Islam would be forever lost.

---

[11] Ibn Tawuus, *Al-Luhuf*, 39-40.

However, after having lost all legitimacy due to perpetrating such a heinous offense, this would no longer be the case. Separating true religious authority from the contemporary political authority was so great a cause that the sacrifice was well worth it. Achieving this mission outweighed any negative repercussions that also transpired.

When the tyrant continues to transgress the boundaries of morality, he only affirms to the nation the illegitimacy of his rule. And the further the tyrant feels that he is not accepted as legitimate, the bolder he will be to commit greater crimes and atrocities. This itself was a great advantage for Islam and the Muslim nation in those circumstances – affirming to the people that the state is not a representative of divine will, but in fact an enemy of it.

The tragedy also deepened the divide between the Shia and the rest of Muslim society. Successive rulers and dynasties all adopted ideologies that were contrary to the school of thought of the Progeny. They all emphasized reverence for the early caliphs, as they were the founders of the caliphate's state and the source of its legitimacy in the mind of the public.

But since the nation had already chosen not to be united in pursuit of what is righteous and true, it is better for it to be divided than to be united in deviance. This is especially true when the true teachings of the faith are openly preached and are available for whoever is willing to seek them out.

## THE PATH OF PROPHETS

This was the path of all prophets, messengers, saints, and reformers. In their call, they came into direct conflict with both state and society. More often than not, their call to God and the truth caused division in their nation. The most successful in this were those who were able to unify their supporters under the banner of truth in the face of an enemy that carried the banner of falsity and deviance.

And in causing such division, the prophets and their successors had clear justification – that they were calling to the truth and guiding people to their Lord. They sought to illuminate the path of truth "So that he who perishes might perish by a manifest proof, and he who lives may live on by a manifest proof."[12]

Prophet Muhammad had to deliver God's revelation despite the division that it would cause. Imam Hussain's rise deepened division between Muslims for the sake of elucidating the faith's true teachings. So what difference is there between the two movements?

If the Prophet had to endure to ensure the rise of a nation that accepts the word of God, Imam Hussain had to endure to ensure there would be those to persevere and protect that word of God.

---

[12] The Holy Quran, 8:42.

## A WEAKENED STATE

Some have attacked Imam Hussain and his revolution, characterizing it as a cause for the weakness of the Muslim or Arab state.

Such a state that is built on tyranny and oppression will inevitably be the target of attack and is in danger of being weakened and destroyed. It is better for the internal struggle to be a struggle between good and evil, so that good cannot be easily ignored and forgotten. Otherwise, internal struggle would ensue, but will be characterized by discord between competing factions vying for power – none of whom care about the faith and its teachings.

From an Islamic perspective, the claim that Imam Hussain's revolution weakened the Arab state is irrelevant at best. In fact, the claim goes back to racial zeal that Islam disparaged.

Of course, a strong Muslim state is important, to a degree. It would be able to protect its citizens and broadcast the true message of Islam to its citizens and to the world. This is why Imam Ali did not fight the early caliphs and claim his right, as discussed earlier.

But this remains important so long as the state is acting in accordance with Islam's true teachings. By now, the reader knows full well that this was not the case. When the state is distorting religion in pursuit of its own twisted goals, it becomes necessary to stop it in its tracks. A stance must be made to elucidate the true teachings of the faith and expose the depravity of the wicked tyrants.

This is what happened in the course of Islamic history by virtue of the stance of the Holy Household of the Prophet.

The climax of that movement was led by Imam Hussain in the battle of Karbala, where he was massacred along with his family and companions.

Imam Hussain's movement was necessary. His movement served the long-term strategic vision of safeguarding the faith's principles for centuries that followed. The Muslim nation was at a critical stage. It was on a trajectory of deviance and corruption that threatened to completely change the identity of Islam. Someone had to take a stance and ensure that the true teachings of the faith are protected. Someone had to rid the state of its perceived legitimacy and stop its meddling in God's religion. Who better to take on that role than the most dedicated person to the principles that had to be saved – Imam Hussain?

# REPERCUSSIONS

The sacrifice at Karbala achieved its intended results. It shook the nation to the core and alerted it to the trajectory of atrophy and degeneration that the state had set it on. It brought about a sudden sense of guilt for allowing such a massacre and not supporting the call of a preeminent reformer in the face of growing corruption.

By this, the foundation upon which the tyrants laid their state was demolished. They lost their legitimacy. They lost their effectiveness in distorting and indoctrinating.

Achieving this goal required the dedicated efforts of some of Islam's greatest personalities. Imam Ali had endured so much in his efforts to preserve the teachings of his cousin and mentor – the Prophet Muhammad. Though some had tried to make the message subservient to the state, Imam Ali stood against their plans and ensured that they do not come to fruition. Imam Hassan carried the banner of his father and stood against Muawiya to guarantee that the call of truth was not buried. But when he lost his supporters and saw that the message can only be preserved through a bitter accord with Muawiya, he conceded.

Imam Hussain continued in the path of his father and his brother. He held fast to his brother's accord, knowing well that it was this agreement that allowed their message to persevere until the opportunity arose. And when it did, Imam Hussain was willing to make the ultimate sacrifice to change the course of history. And on the tenth day of Muharram, 61 AH, Imam Hussain changed history.

## THE COURSE OF HISTORY

The tragedy of Karbala set the nation on a new course, quite distinct from the servility and subjugation of the recent past.

Soon after the massacre, the nation began to rebel against the tyranny of the Umayyad state. Hijaz was the first area to rise in revolt. The people of Medina rose in arms against Yazid, but were massacred in the battle of Harra. In the aftermath of the battle, no sanctity was left undefiled in Medina. The city was plundered, women were raped, and people were forced to pay homage as "slaves and chattel to Yazid."[1]

Abdullah ibn Al-Zubayr also led a revolt in Mecca. The army of Yazid surrounded the city and pelted it with catapults. In that incident, a part of the Grand Mosque and the Holy Kaaba were destroyed.

Yazid did not last long in the seat of power. He died less than four years after accession to the throne. He was so hat-

---

[1] Al-Yaqoubi, *Tareekh Al-Yaqoubi*, 2:250-51.

ed by the Muslim nation that his own governors disparaged him in their eulogies.[2]

Yazid had assigned his son Muawiya II to be successor to the throne. But at the death of his father, Muawiya II took to the pulpit and declared,

> *Surely, my grandfather Muawiya ibn Abu Sufyan challenged someone who was more worthy than him. He [i.e. Imam Ali] was kin to the Messenger of God and more worthy [of leadership] in Islam. He preceded all Muslims and was the first of the faithful. [He was] the cousin of the Messenger of the Lord of the Realms. [He was] the father of the Progeny of the Seal of the Prophets.*
>
> *[Muawiya] then used you in a manner that you surely remember. And you used him in a manner that you do not deny. This until he met his demise and became accountable for his deeds.*
>
> *Then my father was coronated. He was not apt for good, and so he rode on his desires and fancied his mistakes. He had high ambitions, but hope did not comply and life cut him short. He lost any protection, his era ended, and he ascended to his grave where he is accountable for his sins and a prisoner of his crimes.*

He began to weep and said,

> *The worst of it is that we know of his horrid demise and ill fate, after he had murdered the Progeny of the Messenger of God, defiled all sanctity, and burned the Kaaba.*
>
> *But I will not assume your command and bear your sins. Your matter is up to you. By God! If this world were a*

---

[2] Ibn Al-Atheer, *Al-Kamil fe Al-Tareekh*, 4:131.

*treasure, then we have taken our share. And if it were vile,
then the children of Abu Sufyan should suffice themselves
with what they have reaped of it.* [3]

Muawiya II did not live long after that. Historical accounts
differ on when he died, but put it in the range of one[4] to
four months[5] after the death of his father. Some historians
say that he died of a stab wound,[6] while others claim poison
as the cause.[7]

The remainder of the Umayyad clan were so appalled by the
words of Muawiya II that they took revenge on his private
tutor. They claimed that he had taught Muawiya II the love
of Imam Ali and the remainder of the Prophet's family, and
so they buried him alive for this sin.[8]

*Marwanites at the Helm*

With the death of Muawiya II, the dynasty that his grandfather sought to establish came to an end. Though the Umayyad state continued through Muawiya's Marwanite cousins,
his hopes of creating a dynasty for his bloodline did not
come to fruition.

This was not the end of the discord that was brought about
by the ripples of the tragedy of Karbala. It took ten years
for the Marwanites to tighten their grasp on power. They
were forced to deal with continuous rebellions. Some were

---

[3] Al-Yaqoubi, *Tareekh Al-Yaqoubi*, 2:254. See also: Al-Dimyari, *Hayat Al-Haywan*, 112; Ibn Al-Dimashqi, *Jawahir Al-Matalib*, 2:261-62; Al-Isami, *Simt Al-Nujoom Al-Awali*, 3:102.

[4] Al-Balathiri, *Ansaab Al-Ashraaf*, 5:379.

[5] Ibn Asakir, *Tareekh Dimashq*, 59:305.

[6] Ibn Katheer, *Al-Bidaya wa Al-Nihaya*, 8:261.

[7] See, for example: Al-Tabari, *Tareekh Al-Tabari*, 4:409.

[8] Ibn Al-Dimashqi, *Jawahir Al-Matalib*, 2:261-62.

in direct reaction to the tragedy of the massacre in Karbala. Others were led by opportunistic chieftains that saw the time ripe for their grasp for power.

First came the Repenters' Revolt.[9] Then the revolt of Mukhtar.[10] Abdullah ibn Al-Zubayr continued to make mischief, and so did the Kharijites. These were the major movements against the Umayyad state – smaller insurrections continued to pop up here and there.[11]

This was all part of what Lady Fatima had foretold of decades ago when she said,

> [The tree] has been fertilized, so wait until it gives its fruit! You will fill your cauldrons with newly spilt blood and deadly poison. On that day 'the falsifiers will fail'[12] and the wretched will realize the results of what their predecessors established. There, you must let yourselves be comforted away from this world and muster fortitude in the face of sedition. Give tidings to a piercing sword, the tyranny of a repressive aggressor, enveloping pandemonium, and despotism on the

---

[9] Many people that did not participate in the battle of Karbala felt the sting of regret. Most of these individuals were not able to join Imam Hussain because they were imprisoned or otherwise prevented by ibn Ziyad, the governor of Kufa. Still, they felt the need to 'repent' for not having supported Imam Hussain in his cause and rose in rebellion after the massacre. Their movement was dubbed the Repenters' Revolt – *Thawrat Al-Tawwabeen.*

[10] Al-Mukhtar ibn Abu Ubayd Al-Thaqafi, a notable amongst the Shia of the period. He led a revolt in the wake of the massacre at Karbala. The revolt was ultimately defeated by the forces of the Umayyad government and Abdullah ibn Al-Zubayr. –Eds.

[11] Al-Yaqoubi, *Tareekh Al-Yaqoubi*, 2:263.

[12] The Holy Quran, 45:27.

*side of oppressors that will leave your livelihoods meager and your band an [easy] harvest.[13]*

## Twelve Years of Turmoil

Twelve years of turmoil followed the massacre of Karbala. It was not until the defeat of Abdullah ibn Al-Zubayr in the year 73 AH that Abdulmalik ibn Marwan was able to tighten his grasp on power.

This period of turmoil was significant for two main reasons.

### Stripping the State of Legitimacy

This period clearly showcased the state's degeneracy and distance from any set of morals and principles. This was most evidently true in the final victors of this struggle – the Marwanite branch of the Umayyad clan. The Marwanites had no known quality or achievement that would qualify them for leadership. They were, in fact, the most unqualified for the position, as they were known for their immorality and impiety. This led to the complete loss of legitimacy and respect for the religious pretentions of the state.

Thus, it became evident that, in such circumstances, making an oath of allegiance to the state did not mean giving it any legitimacy. The concept of *taqiyya* became evident to the public, due mostly to the efforts of the Progeny. And as the caliphs and the caliphate continued to degenerate, people began to realize that allegiance given under duress is by no means a sign of true allegiance or legitimacy.

Of course, this also meant that an alteration to the ideology of the masses was in order. Scholars finally began to admit

---

[13] Ibn Tayfour, *Balaghat Al-Nisa*, 19-20.

that obedience to such a state is not a religious obligation, especially when its commands directly contradict the commands of God. They thus began to shed the weight of the great multitude of fabrications and distortions that had taken hold before.

It also became abundantly clear that there was no obligation to sustain the unity of the nation under the leadership of the caliph – as was the dominant ideology before the tragedy of Karbala. Rather, the public began to realize that the divine command for unity meant only unity in the cause of truth. Still, many scholars amongst the public continued to stress the religious obligation to pay allegiance to the caliph. This created some confusion amongst the public, as can be imagined.

With all this, the opposition to the state was no longer considered a religious misdeed. Opposition was no longer the domain of the Kharijites and the Shia. Rather, there were many amongst the opposition who were regarded as part of the Muslim mainstream, respected and looked up to by the vast majority of the public.

In turn, this stripped the state of all its religious pretensions. The first era of the caliphate was marked by an equation of religious and political authority in the minds of the public. The state held the power to dictate religion. But after the halo of legitimacy was dismantled, the state was no longer seen as the arbiter of religious query. The caliphate became wholly and exclusively a political affair. Brutality was no longer a means to dictating religion, but only to establishing political authority.

## Renewed Freedom

These twelve years of turmoil also broke some of the shackles that the state had imposed on the nation. Most importantly, there was a renewed freedom of thought throughout the nation. This did not come because the state stopped persecuting people with ideas contrary to state ideology. Rather, it was the rise of widespread defiance to the state that made it impractical for the state to enforce its own ideology strictly across the territories of the caliphate. Thus, its policies of enforcement lessened and freedom of thought increased.

Thus, a new era of religious diversity emerged. This was most prominently due to the efforts of the Shia in propagating their principles and ideology. After all, it was their Imam who had been murdered in Karbala and whose tragedy upturned life and society in the Muslim nation. Of course, Imam Hussain was not only the religious leader of the Shia, he was the most revered and respected religious leader in the nation – else he would have simply been rejected as the leader of a fringe faction.

The prominence of the Shia's religious leadership did not stop with Imam Hussain. The tradition continued with his children after him. Their preeminence in society was the reason for the spread of their school of thought. They were regarded as the heirs to the Prophet's knowledge and the gates of his wisdom.

# IMPACT

It is no surprise then that the tragedy of Karbala had a profound impact on the Muslim nation. It shook the conscience of the nation and allowed it to reflect on its present state. It brought Muslims back to the true teachings of the Prophet and allowed them to doff the shackles of state ideology.

Muslims were shaken by the tragedy because it allowed them to finally see the baneful trajectory that the Umayyads had set them on. The Progeny and their devoted followers continued to remind the Muslims of the tragedy of Karbala and kept its memory ever present in the conscience of society. They continued to mourn Imam Hussain every year, commemorating the day of his sacrifice. To this day, they continue to remember the sacrifice that he made and the impact that it had on the nation. Upon hearing the story of Imam Hussain, any Muslim of sound mind and heart would flock back to the faith and reject the corruption of the Umayyads.

The daily struggle of Muslims under the subjugation of the state also became apparent. The nation was in constant turmoil, as warring factions fought over political power. The ordinary Muslim found no refuge but in retreating away from public life and focusing on self, faith, and family. Interestingly, with the blatant deviance of political leaders, personal devotion and piety became a form of defiance and opposition to the tyranny of the state.

In all this, the Shia continued to be the vanguard of change. The Shia used the renewed vigor and strength that the tragedy of Karbala gave them to spread the true teachings of Islam. They combined their devotion to the conceptual framework of Islam with an equal devotion to practical application of religious teachings. They were known to be the most pious and learned.[14] This became a tool for the Shia to spread the original teachings of the Prophet, as they led by example and spread knowledge of theology, law, and ethics.

## A CLEAR RELIGIOUS FRAMEWORK

Once the state's jurisdiction over religion was dismantled, the nation felt the need for a religious authority that would instruct the laity on the matters of their faith. Thus, the nation began to foster specialists in religious teachings and understanding.

Such a group did exist in the first half-century after the death of the Prophet. It consisted mostly of companions of the Prophet and disciples of Imam Ali. Yet they were often unable to take the role of religious guidance and leadership because of state persecution and the nation's intolerance to any ideology that contradicted government propaganda.

But after the dismantling of the state's religious guise and the effectual separation between religion and state in the mind of the public, this class of religious specialists began to grow more effective and influential. It adopted diverse opinions and a multitude of approaches. They grew in numbers and began to specialize as narrators of prophetic traditions, Quranic exegetes, jurists, ascetics, mystics, and preachers.

---

[14]Al-Asfahani, *Maqatil Al-Talibiyyin*, 195.

They created an effective religious authority outside state structures.

As always, the Shia were at the forefront of the trend. They had devoted themselves to the path of Imam Ali and his sons – the family of the Prophet and the heirs to his knowledge and wisdom.

The Shia imposed their presence in this way. Even al-Dhahabi, a revered Sunni scholar, would say that "If the traditions narrated by these men were to be rejected, a significant portion of prophetic heritage would be lost. This would surely be an obvious misfortune."[15] Al-Jawzajani, with his blatant enmity towards the Shia, would also say that they were "the head narrators of Kufa… people tolerated them for their truthful tongues in narration" despite their differing ideology.[16]

In any case, history led to the creation of a class of religious scholars and experts with a diverse set of ideologies and schools of thought. Competition amongst scholars began to form, either because of a sincere interest to find the truth, or for the sake of fame and power or other worldly pursuits.

In all this diversity, one proposition emerged as an undisputed fact – religious authority is limited to the Quran and the tradition, without any right for the state or anyone else to intrude. Even if other sources are proposed as legitimately authoritative in religious matters, their legitimacy would have to be drawn from the Quran or the prophetic traditions.

---

[15] Al-Dhahabi, *Mizan Al-I'tidal*, 1:5.
[16] Al-Jawzajani, *Ahwal Al-Rijal*, 78-80.

Scholarly debate continued around these sources until jurisprudence became an accepted and studied science. For the Muslim nation, such an advance was unprecedented especially due to the fact that the state had no hand in the development.

The state began to interact with this phenomenon in an effort to coopt it into the state structure, or at least limit its divergence against state interests. The political establishment first attempted to control the process of documenting prophetic traditions, after having banned the practice for so long. The state also adopted its own jurists, establishing a system of patronage that was meant to restore religious legitimacy.

The door of error and corruption amongst religious leaders was always open. But this did not outweigh the benefit of the state's affirmative acceptance of the Quran and prophetic tradition as the ultimate authority in religion. The caliph no longer held an unbridled authority to alter and distort the faith.

In all this, the teachings of the religion remained safe. All Muslims agreed that the ultimate authority in religion is the word of God as inscribed in the Holy Quran and the prophetic traditions that were carved into the hearts and minds of the Muslims.

### Reverence for the 'Rightly Guided'

What remained is the issue of the religious authority of the tradition of the first two 'Rightly Guided Caliphs.' The majority of the public continued to hold them in such high regard bordering on sanctification. Some schools of thought attempted to list it as a primary source of religious authority, in line with the Quran and the prophetic tradition.

Imam Ali had repeatedly spoken against such undue reverence. Recall, for example, that he had rejected to accept leadership after the death of Omar because it was conditioned on following the precedent of the first two caliphs. Imam Ali's sons continued in the same vein.

The Progeny and their followers insisted that religious authority lied primarily and fundamentally in the Quran and the prophetic tradition. In the end, their view won out. Although the majority of the nation still held on to the tradition of the first two caliphs, they acquiesced that it was secondary to the Quran and tradition.

The discussion thereafter revolved around the sources which held authoritative value only secondarily – that is, sources that are only authoritative because the Quran and the prophetic tradition give them authority. It is in this discussion that the majority of differences among Muslim schools of thought begin to emerge.

Yet, this debate is not of great consequential value in the general trajectory of the Muslim nation. The Quran and the prophetic traditions remained supreme, and a seeker of truth is free to choose amongst the sects based on evidence and proof. Not only did the existential threat to Islam subside, this new framework of scholarly debate allowed for the propagation of Islam's true teachings.

All this was due to the efforts of the Progeny and their sacrifices – especially the sacrifice of Imam Hussain. The tragedy of Karbala had changed the course of the nation. It shook the nation to its core and brought it back to its conscience. Because of the tragedy of Karbala, opposition to the state and calls for reform began to echo across the nation. It put an end to state manipulation and distortion of religion.

The religion of Islam was saved from the threat of annihilation or complete distortion by the sacrifice of Imam Hussain in Karbala.

# LEGACY

There is another set of implications that are of great significance to the study of the tragedy of Karbala. Imam Hussain's sacrifice and the sacrifices of the Progeny built a legacy for their followers and devotees. Their school of thought – the school of Shia Islam – was the legacy of their sacrifice.

The Progeny gave their followers a wealth of knowledge, textual evidence, and logical arguments to support their faith. But the Progeny also gave their followers a legacy that is emotionally charged. The leaders of the Shia – the family of the Prophet – were revered by all Muslims. Yet they faced the greatest of oppression and made the greatest sacrifices in preserving the faith. The most evident example is, of course, that of Imam Hussain in Karbala.

## EVIDENCE

The Shia reaped great benefits from the legacy of their leaders in the field of knowledge and textual evidence. As the curators of the Quran and the prophetic traditions, the Progeny delivered to their followers a strong sense of connection to these sources and a keen ability to decipher their meanings.

It is amazing that divine compassion has preserved so much textual evidence that supports the school of thought of the Progeny, despite the persecution of their followers and the conscious efforts to obscure their heritage. If any researcher would approach the text objectively and doff the accumulated prejudices of the past, the veracity of Shia beliefs would be abundantly apparent.

The Shia claimed a unique victory through the short term impacts of the tragedy of Karbala. They had long asserted that the Quran and the prophetic traditions were the only legitimate sources of religious authority. Their view was solidified across the Muslim nation as a result of the tragedy.

*Ebbing the Tides*

This is why the enemies of the Progeny and their devotees had to resort to twisted means to stop the growth of this school of thought. Harassment and persecution of the Shia continued as it had throughout the history of the caliphate's state. In addition, the state and its patron scholars attempted to defame the Shia and hold them out to be polytheists and apostates. By these lies, they hoped to isolate the Shia from the general populace and ebb the rising tide of Shia Islam.

In addition, they tried to insulate the public from the thoughts and ideas of the Progeny and their followers. They warned the public not to interact or engage in a dialogue or debate with any Shia, as it could be detrimental to a believer's faith. They presented their own religious ideology as well established and indisputable. Even in religious discussions, the perspective of the Shia was often overlooked. In spite of all this, they were still apprehensive about discussing any literature or evidence that supported the Shia perspective.

*Clarifying Legitimacy*

Prior to the tragedy of Karbala, the state had provided ample evidence – mostly through distortion – for the public to believe that the caliphs held legitimate authority over the nation.

The public willfully ignored Imam Ali's reluctance in pledging allegiance to Abu Bakr – rather, his initial rejection of his caliphate. They tried to make justifications for his stance that would give legitimacy to the state.

They willfully ignored the stance of Lady Fatima, who died shortly after a dispute with the first caliph and had undoubtedly rejected the legitimacy of his bid for power.

They willfully ignored the stance of Imam Hassan and misrepresented his motives in signing his bitter accord with Muawiya – accusing him of cowardice and opportunism.

But they could not ignore Imam Hussain's stance in Karbala. The gravity of the tragedy did not allow them to do so. Thus, they had to explain it in one of two ways. Either recognize the justification of Imam Hussain's actions at the expense of stripping legitimacy from Yazid. Or legitimize Yazid's rule and actions by delegitimizing Imam Hussain's movement.

Neither of these possibilities properly fit the framework of state propagated ideology. This left much confusion in the minds of the public. Most decided to simply skirt the issue.

Nonetheless, it was a grand victory for Shia Islam because the objective observer could clearly see where truth and justice lied.

## EMOTION

The Shia had gained the honor of being at the forefront of the nation's martyrs. They were the closest aides to the Prophet and to Imam Ali. They were part of the greatest tragedy in the history of Islam – rather the greatest tragedy in the history of revealed religions.

And if we look closely at the words and actions of Imam Hussain and his companions, we would see that their movement had a decidedly Shia outlook. They sought to instill the idea of the Progeny's preeminence and divine right. Imam Hussain had told his half-brother Muhammad ibn Al-Hanafiyya before leaving Medina,

> *I do not revolt due to discontent, nor out of arrogance. I did not rise as a corruptor, nor as an oppressor. Rather, I wish to call for reform in the nation of my grandfather. I wish to call for what is good, and to forbid what is evil. [I wish to] follow the tradition of my grandfather [the Prophet] and my father Imam Ali ibn Abu Talib.[1]*

And in his letter to the heads of the five major tribes in Basra, he wrote,

> *Surely, God chose Muhammad over his creations, honored him with prophecy, and selected him for His message. God then took his soul to Himself, after he had counseled God's*

---

[1] Al-Bahrani, *Al-Awalim*, 179.

*servants and delivered the message that he was given. We
were his family, successors, vicegerents, and heirs – and the
ones most worthy of his position amongst people. Our people
then favored [others] over us, yet we contented out of dislike
for disunity and desire for the wellbeing [of the nation]. This
is while we know that we are more worthy of that right that
was due to us than the ones that had taken it....*[2]

And there is much more evidence to support this view, especially in Imam Hussain's correspondence with the people
of Kufa and Lady Zaynab's sermons after the massacre.[3]

*Commemorating the Tragedy*

The scholars of the Muslim public realized all this. They saw
that if Imam Hussain's call was to be heeded and remembered, it would mean stripping away all legitimacy from the
state – not just the state of the Umayyad clan and their successors, but of the early caliphs. And since they held a reverence that bordered sanctification for these individuals,
they could not stand idle as Imam Hussain's movement
continue in remembrance.

And thus we see that many Muslim scholars that do not ascribe to the school of thought of the Progeny discourage
remembrance and commemoration of the tragedy, despite
their knowledge of its gravity. As Al-Ghazali said,

*It is impermissible for a preacher or anyone else to recite the
story of Hussain's massacre and narration of what had occurred between the companions of disputes and enmity. That
would surely incite detestation of the companions and criti-*

---

[2] Al-Tabari, *Tareekh Al-Tabari*, 4:266.
[3] See, for example: Al-Khawarizmi, *Maqtal Al-Hussain*, 63-64.

*cism of them. Yet they are the notables of the religion. The disputes amongst them must be correctly rationalized. It may perhaps be due to an error in judgment, rather than a pursuit of power or affluence.*[4]

Sa'daldeen Al-Taftazani also wrote,

*As for what occurred of oppression towards the family of the Prophet, it is so apparent that it cannot be hidden. It is so vile that opinions cannot disagree about [condemning] it. Surely, even inanimate objects and wild beasts would attest to this if they could... So let the damnation of God befall whoever initiated, was content with, or supported [this oppression] – 'and the punishment of the Hereafter is more severe and lasting.*[5]

*What if it were to be said 'there are scholars of the sect that prohibit the cursing of Yazid,' despite their knowledge that he deserves this and much more? We would say that they said this to prevent an escalation to the more superior, as is the call of the Rawafid as recited in their supplications and gatherings.*

*Therefore, those who cared about the status of the religion saw that they should reign in the public with such ambiguity. It was a way for conservatism in belief so that feet do not slip from balance and minds do not deviate due to desire.*

*Otherwise, who would deny the permissibility and the justification? And how could it not be an issue of unanimity.*[6]

All this did not harm the Shia, but inadvertently advanced their cause. By attempting to justify the actions of men like

---

[4] Al-Barusawi, *Rooh Al-Bayan*, 8:24.
[5] The Holy Quran, 20:127.
[6] *Al-Taftazani*, Sharh Al-Maqasid, 2:306-07.

Yazid, state sponsored scholars only brought skepticism to their ideology. Anyone who justified these actions became constructively complicit to the crime. Such attempts only showed the irreverence and even hatred that some held to-ward the family of the Prophet.

## HERITAGE

The horror of the tragedy of Karbala set the groundwork for the Shia to spread their teachings. They used the com-memorations of the massacre – an event that all Muslims related to – as a platform for broadcasting their views on the status and right of the Progeny, as well as the villainous nature of their oppressors.

From the commemorations of the tragedy of Karbala, the Shia began to grow. And as they grew, they commemorated and celebrated the legacy of all the members of the Progeny.

All this drew the ire of successive generations of tyrannical caliphs. They intensified their efforts of harassment and persecution against the followers of the Progeny.

This did not discourage the Shia. They carried the legacy of the Progeny – a legacy of oppression and persecution. Per-secution by the state only made them stronger. It added to their resilience and determination. It intensified their devo-tion.

Persecution by the state could not stop the Shia rituals of commemoration. It only deepened the Shia's conviction of the importance of these rituals. And as generations passed and the struggle with the state continued, these rituals be-came more integral to the Shia identity.

*Engagement*

The rituals and heritage of commemoration had a great impact on the development of Shia Islam. For one, it allowed the Shia to remain engaging and effective.

The Shia sect remained lively and active due to this. They continued to commemorate the tragedy of Hussain every year. Even more, they began to commemorate and celebrate the significant events relating to the Progeny. And as can be seen throughout history and even in modern times, their commemorations are often attention grabbing and awe-inspiring.

This proved to be a remarkable tool for the disseminating the teachings of the Progeny. Although commemorations have an unmistakable emotional dimension, such gatherings could not go without an intellectual dimension as well. Thus, the Shia remained, generally speaking, more educated in the manners of their faith than the remainder of the Muslim nation. The constant remembrance of the Prophet, his family, and the teachings of the faith surely had impact on listeners in these events. Thus, the Shia became known further for their piety, knowledge, and honesty. [7]

The call of the Shia rose and echoed. Their consistent and continuous commemorations and celebrations peeked the interests of many. Their unapologetic devotion to the Progeny and stance in the face of oppression fascinated observers. Thus, the Shia were able to engage the rest of the Muslim public and showcase to them their heritage and ideology. The Shia continued to grow in strength and numbers.

---

[7] See, for example: Al-Asfahani, *Maqatil Al-Talibiyyin*, 195.

## Unity

The rituals of commemoration also unified the Shia in a common cause and strengthened their bond through remembrance of the oppression of their leaders. They were united in their devotion to the Progeny and opposition to their oppressors.

This unity wasn't just conceptual and theoretical. Rather, it became material as the Shia were physically and spiritually engaged in commemoration and celebration. Take, for example, their eagerness to contribute time, effort, and resources to their cause. They built mosques and community centers where they gathered to sing the praises of the Progeny.

They built schools and places of worship in the name of the Prophet Muhammad. They fed the poor and destitute in the name of Imam Ali. They cared for the orphans in the name of Lady Fatima. They tended to the sick and the wayfarer in the name of Imam Hassan. They established commemorations and shed tears in the name of Imam Hussain.

This environment of shared emotions and a shared cause brought the Shia closer together. Across the nation, the Shia remained well knit and united.

## Identity

The tragedy also had a great impact in solidifying the Shia identity. The rituals of commemoration and supplication, and the visitation of sanctified graves and holy shrines, all imbedded a unique sense of identity in the Shia Muslim. Despite harassment and persecution, the Shia were able to hold tight to that identity.

Thus, the Shia could not be summed up by their scholars and religious leaders. The school of thought could not be eliminated simply by eliminating its leaders. It remained deeply embedded in the hearts and minds of every follower of the Shia creed. Devotion to the Progeny was no ritualistic practice – it was an identity.

Persecution and harassment no longer served as deterrents. They became a source of strength for this identity. As the Progeny was persecuted and oppressed, so were their followers and devotees. Hardship strengthened the Shia connection to their divine principles and immaculate leaders. This is why, despite the numerous attempts throughout history, the devotees of the Progeny could not be eliminated.

The tragedy of Karbala played a great role in the creation of this identity. Thus, it had a quintessential role in the preservation of the Shia faith throughout time. It may even be said that these commemorations were the formidable defense which kept the Shia faith alive and well.

## WATERSHED

Hussain's movement and massacre in Karbala became a watershed for the Shia. It gave the school of thought renewed vigor and strength. It intensified devotion to the Progeny and solidified the identity of the believers. It elucidated the call of Prophet and his family and allowed it to rise without the corruption and distortion of the state.

God the Almighty said,

> *Have you not regarded how God has drawn a parable? A good word is like a good tree: its roots are steady and its*

*branches are in the sky. It gives its fruit every season by the leave of its Lord. God draws these parables for mankind so that they may take admonition.[8]*

These words are befitting of the sacrifice of Imam Hussain – a man of patience, perseverance, fortitude, and contentment with the will of his Lord.

This is why Imam Hussain would be go on to write,

*Surely, whoever follows me will be martyred. Whoever does not follow me will not witness the triumph.[9]*

---

[8] The Holy Quran, 14:24-25.
[9] Al-Qummi, *Kamil Al-Ziyarat*, 157.

# MEANS AND ENDS

Anyone who looks closely at the movement of Imam Hussain will see clearly that he aimed to preserve the noblest of values and greatest of principles. It was important for him to be clear about his goals, as he aimed to show the nation how to act with clarity and vision.

We saw this from Imam Hussain in his conversations in Medina. He would tell his half-brother Muhammad ibn Al-Hanafiyya, for example, exactly where he was headed, why he was going there, and the details of the ensuing tragedy. In the same vein, he declared to anyone who opposed him that he will take patience as a weapon and wait until God's judgment is done. Imam Hussain would say,

> *I do not revolt due to discontent, nor out of arrogance. I did not rise as a corruptor, nor as an oppressor. Rather, I wish to call for reform in the nation of my grandfather. I wish to call for what is good, and to forbid what is evil... Whoever accepts me because I carry the truth, then God is the refuge of the honest. As for whoever rejects this call, I will be pa-*

*tient until God judges between me and the rejecters with His justice. Surely, He is the best of judges.[1]*

He would candidly write,

*Surely, whoever follows me will be martyred. Whoever does not follow me will not witness the triumph.[2]*

## THE MEANS

The means to achieving a noble end must be fitting and reciprocal in nobility and uprightness.

There are some who would say that such noble standards are too ideal. They claim that trickery must be met with trickery and that the reformer must out-deceive the state in order to effectuate real change. The ends justify the means.

This is clearly an erroneous opinion.

Let us assume, for argument's sake, that such devious means would achieve the same goals. Would it be worth it? Clearly not. It is better to limit the movement of reform to what is practicable than to stray outside the bounds of morality and virtue in order to pursue reforms that are purportedly greater. When some of Imam Ali's companions would suggest some twisted ways for him to combat his enemies, he would chastise them saying, "I do not see that I should reform you by corrupting myself."[3]

In fact, standing by principle and avoiding all corrupt methods is itself a method of reform in the long term. This was

---

[1] Al-Bahrani, *Al-Awalim*, 179.
[2] Al-Qummi, *Kamil Al-Ziyarat*, 157.
[3] Al-Balathiri, *Ansaab Al-Ashraaf*, 3:215.

the Progeny's approach to reform the nation. The end did not justify the means. Rather, it was of the utmost importance to pursue the noble ends by the right means, even if standing by these principles meant short-term setbacks. In that, they were not simply pursuing noble ends, but practically applying nobility and virtue in their actions – despite all the sacrifices that had to be given.

By this, they showed the nation that nobility and virtue are not just idealistic concepts, but practical qualities that must be fulfilled. The Progeny did not suffice themselves with coining catchy slogans on justice, patience, sacrifice, and all other virtues. They implemented these values in their lives. They gave the greatest sacrifices to show the nation that they are tangible and attainable.

The lesson here is that anyone who calls for reform but goes about his stated mission through twisted means cannot be trusted. Such an individual is either too weak to stand by principle and will quickly swerve away from the path of truth. Or he does not care for principle in the first place and his call for 'reform' is only a bid for power or some other personal ambition.

In fact, such an individual may only further corruption rather than achieve any reform. Once the floodgates of excuses and justifications are opened, they are difficult to close.

Assume again, for argument's sake, that we adopt the idea that 'the ends do justify the means' and allow the perpetration of crimes in the name of a noble cause. Little by little, we will grow accustomed to crimes in the name of the cause. The weight of crimes will diminish. In the long term, this would mean the incremental acceptance of justified vice, then an acceptance of vice altogether. With this, the purported purpose of reform would be undone.

## THE ENDS

As we discussed before, Imam Ali's tenure as caliph revealed the impracticability of achieving a completely reformed Muslim state – one that would implement the teachings of Islam to their fullest. Yet this did not discourage the Shia from pursuing reform.

The Shia of Kufa were especially adamant, as they felt a sense of guilt for letting Imam Ali down. They were willing to bear any burden and persevere against all odds to achieve the mission of reform. However, in their eagerness, they lost sight of the bigger picture. As alleged reformers came and went, they could not accurately assess whether they were being led by true men of principles or by an opportunistic bunch.

Because of this, they began to badger Imam Hassan and Imam Hussain to rise in arms against Muawiya. But the grandsons of the Prophet refused. They knew that the stage was not yet set for what they were being asked. They knew that rising at the time would lead to their martyrdoms, a tragedy that would not have the necessary impact at the time given the circumstances.

And when Muawiya passed, the Shia saw an opportune time for the promised revolution and reform. They made promises to Imam Hussain and asked him to come to Kufa. Yet they shirked in their promises, and the result was the grievous massacre.

Imam Hussain answered the call and rose for the protection of the faith. But he did not have the same goals as the petitioners in Kufa. He knew that he had set on a journey of sacrifice. All they wanted was change to the political system.

## Unattainable Reforms

The tragedy of Karbala confirmed once again that the reforms people asked for could not be attained – much like the experience of Imam Ali revealed years before. In fact, as time passed, these reforms became more and more impractical. This was most evident to the public after the massacre of Karbala.

Imam Hussain was extraordinary in his character. He was the most knowledgeable of the true nature of Islam. He possessed all the admirable qualities of a righteous leader. He was firm, resolute, just, clement, visionary and principled. In addition, he was the grandson of the Prophet – a title no one could claim but his brother Imam Hassan who was poisoned by Muawiya years earlier. He held an unparalleled preeminence amongst the Muslims.

Time itself also played a role. Even as Imam Hussain made his stance in the year 61 AH, time was incessantly chipping at the collective memory of the Muslim nation. Fifty years may not seem to be a long time in the grand scheme of things. But those fifty years had seen the passing of many men who had seen and heard the Prophet firsthand. The closest of the Prophet's disciples and companions were withering away. It wouldn't take much longer for that generation of disciples to be entirely gone.

The nation was on a trajectory of degeneration that was not easily reversible. Especially because of Umayyad control of the state, the Muslim nation was set on a path of deviance and corruption. The enemies of Islam – embodied in the Umayyad clan – were sitting at the helm of the nation. That itself was a great travesty that the Muslims reluctantly accepted. But as time passed, Umayyad authority was normalized in the public psyche. With passing generations, the fact that the Umayyad clan had taken the helm no longer seemed to be such a tragedy.

There was also a group of devotees that were willing to make the ultimate sacrifice alongside Hussain. This does not include everyone who wrote to him from Kufa and elsewhere calling him to revolt. Amongst these petitioners were opportunists that simply thought they could get a piece of the spoils once he triumphed against the Umayyads. Others were simpletons that moved with the wave of the masses and repeated the calls of whomever they felt affinity towards in the moment.

Rather, the group of devotees that made reform seem somewhat plausible were the ones who sincerely believed in Imam Hussain's mission – a number that was relatively large. A portion of these devotees died alongside him in the massacre of Karbala. But the majority could not make this stance due to extraneous circumstances. Many were imprisoned. Others were captured on their way to Imam Hussain. Some faltered in a moment of weakness when the going got tough or when Imam Hussain's military defeat seemed inevitable.

Despite all this, Imam Hussain's revolt was doomed to a military defeat. He was let down by his supporters and betrayed by many. He knew full well that he was being led to the slaughter. But if meeting this fate meant that he can deliver his message of reform and fulfill his divine mission, then he would oblige without hesitation. He would tell his companions,

> *People are slaves to this world and religion is only words on their tongues. They hold on to it so long as their livelihoods are secured. But if they are tested with tribulation the true believers will be less...*[4]

He would also tell his companions, "I do not see death [for God's sake] except as happiness, and life with these oppressors except as weariness."[5]

Regardless, the Umayyad state continued with its deviance, culminating with the tragedy at Karbala. If anything, the fact that such a tragedy occurred should be enough proof that complete reform was unattainable. The opportunity will never repeat itself. Muslims could not aspire for a leader of the stature of Imam Hussain. Neither could they hope for the emergence of devotees like those of his time. And as time passed on, complete reform proved to be more and more unattainable.

*Emotional Tides*

The emotional tides of the public are not reliable. They ebb and flow across time. They rise when the public tastes the bitterness of corruption and deviance, and grows thirsty for

---

4 Al-Khawarizmi, *Maqtal Al-Hussain*, 1:236-37.
5 Ibn Tawuus, *Al-Luhuf*, 48.

reform. But it quickly ebbs due to fear, false hopes, weariness, and weakness.

Even if we can assume that an opportunity could arise where a military victory is achievable and total reform is attainable, there is no guarantee that such a victory could be sustainable. In fact, what we have seen only convinces us that such a victory would soon be overturned, as it cannot be sustained without transgression against the very principles that reforms are aimed to achieve. Such a reform movement would either be snipped in the bud – as was done with Imam Ali's movement when he was assassinated in the year 40 AH – or gradually eroded and distorted until it loses its defining character.

*Partial Reform*

With this, the only remaining viable option was partial reform. This could be on a personal level, through raising a good family and providing good advice when the opportunity arises. It can also be on a collective level through stemming the rise of corruption in society.

Of course, there has to be a religious justification for any movement. There must also be a cost-benefit analysis that would ensure a movement does not do more harm than good. This, of course, changes across circumstances and depends on the individual's perspective.

Such a reform movement should not be based on catchy slogans and emotional mobilization. It must be thought out carefully and limited only to the proper means that would achieve the greatest success. Again, the ends do not justify the means.

Imam Ali, Imam Hassan, and Imam Hussain knew this very well. This is why their movements were not aimed at a complete reformation of the Muslim nation. Rather, each of them had a goal of partial reform in society in specific ways.

And as we have seen, they were able to achieve these partial reforms by diminishing corruption in the nation and raising the banner of truth for all who can see. By this, they changed the trajectory of society and allowed it to reflect on its own ills. The consequence was the preservation of the faith.

The Shia had not realized all this before the tragedy of Karbala. They were resolute in their opposition to corruption, deviance, and injustice. They had lived in the bitter shadows of Umayyad subjugation for too long. But it all became abundantly clear in the aftermath of the massacre.

*Peace*

The tragedy of Karbala created such a shock for the Shia that they quickly realized the folly of their previous way of thinking. This is why they continued to acquiesce to the Progeny's peaceful stance. After the tragedy of Karbala, the immaculate leaders of the Shia – the Progeny of Muhammad – maintained a peaceful stance and urged their followers to sheathe their swords and maintain the peace. The Shia had incessantly petitioned Imam Ali, Imam Hassan, and Imam Hussain to act. But after the tragedy, they came to see the wisdom of the Progeny's stance.

The Progeny's calls for peace became a rallying cry. It set them apart from others, such as the Fatimids, who simply wanted to establish a state in lieu of the tyrannical caliphate.

In fact, these calls of peace insured the continued perseverance of the Progeny and greater admiration for them in the eyes of the public.

Objection to the Progeny's stance was no longer a normal phenomenon. Though it did occur, it was only in isolated instances that could easily be answered or cured. This was partly due to the fact that the Shia had gained a deeper understanding of their creed, especially the meaning of the 'immaculate' nature of the Progeny.

The tragedy of Karbala had thus removed a burden from the Progeny. They no longer needed to contend with their followers' incessant objections and calls for revolt. It made it easier for them to convince their followers that any revolt is fated for failure.

The Progeny was thus able to spend their efforts on developing their followers and devotees intellectually, away from the chaos of politics. This in itself was a great achievement of the tragedy of Karbala.

*Complete Faith*

The completion of the Muslim religion was conditioned upon the oversight of the Prophet and his rightful successors. As divine appointed guardians of the faith and truly immaculate individuals, they were most apt to safeguard the religion as delivered by the Messenger.

If the early Muslims, both *Muhajiroon* and *Ansar*, had set aside their ambitions and acquiesced to the leadership of its rightful holders, the history of Islam would have been much different. Successorship to the Prophet would have been, in the manner decreed by God, a right held by the Progeny of the Prophet. Beginning with Imam Ali, as the first rightful heir of the Prophet, their rule would have been a true extension of the Prophet's leadership.

Imam Ali was not only the Prophet's nearest of kin. He was the greatest of his supporters. He was at the forefront of every battle and debate. He would speak on behalf of the Prophet in his absence. He carried the same qualities of resolve, determination, knowledge, and virtue.

All this meant that, had Imam Ali been given the reins of political leadership, the seeds of discord and disunity would not have been sowed in the first place. The so-called Wars of Apostasy would not have occurred since the Muslims of the time would have eagerly acquiesced to Imam Ali's rightful claim to successorship. His reign would have diminished all ambitions for political power and therefore prevented many ensuing wars within the Muslim nation. He would have put the hypocrites in their place and prevented any distortion to the faith. He would have strengthened only the most righteous of the companions of the Prophet who devoted themselves to the true message of Islam.

Thus, Islam would have continued to grow and its true teachings would expand to the corners of the earth. Fabrications and distortions would have no place in the Muslim narrative. The nation would reach the zenith of knowledge and piety that God ordained for it had it obeyed His commands.

As Lady Fatima would say soon after her father's death,

> *And thus God had made for you faith so that you may be purified from disbelief, prayer for your transcendence [away*

*from] arrogance… and obedience to us as a framework for*
*creed, and our leadership as a safeguard against disunity…*[6]

Even if some wretched souls rose in rebellion after all this, their danger would quickly be averted as the nation gathers in unity behind its rightful leader. This is how history would have looked had that fateful error not occurred in the formative years of Islam.

## Intractable Deviation

Complete reform became unattainable, as we said earlier, when the nation made its decision to deviate on the first day after the Prophet's demise. The result was the manipulation of religion and isolation of the faith's most loyal devotees. And as the hypocrites took the reins of power, disunity and discord ensued. The alleged position of 'successorship to the Prophet' became nothing but a political ambition sought by tribal chieftains, until it settled in the hands of Islam's sworn enemies.

As a result, a plethora of sects and ideologies emerged. With the true teachings of Islam no longer clear, people resorted to their flawed opinions and whimsical desires in interpreting the religion. The floodgates were opened for purported justification. The Muslims strayed away from textual evidence. The nation was led into a cycle of misrepresentation and transgression in the name of faith. But it soon grew acclimated to the situation.

---

[6] Ibn Tayfour, *Balaghat Al-Nisa*, 14.

## The Occultation

The complexity of this situation is only aggravated during the occultation of the Twelfth Imam from the Progeny of the Prophet.

The Immaculate Imam is no longer accessible to the Muslims who wish to receive his direct verbal instructions on matters of their faith. Instead, they are left with religious scholars who are tasked with deducing the true teachings of Islam from its authoritative sources. There is no doubt that these scholars are at risk of erring in their deductions – the fact that they disagree is a testament to the fact that they do.

Add to this the plethora of religious, non-religious, and anti-religious ideologies that come and go with the passing years. And as time goes on, the situation of the sickly human society only increases in complexity. Problems only become more abundant and more aggravated. Still, the fact that total reformation is unattainable should not discourage the nation to seek something partial and incremental.

And as should be abundantly clear, these tragedies did not come to be because of some deficiency in the revelation or a flaw in the religious system. Rather, the nation had brought all this unto itself through its own choices. It allowed for deviance and degeneracy to take hold and did not fulfill its obligation of reform in those formative years. The nation bore the impact of these decisions, and it will continue to carry the burden of its sins.

# IMAM ALI'S LEGACY

It is evident that all the Imams of the Progeny shared in the responsibility of taking care of the religion and struggled to preserve and protect it. Imam Hussain was not the only one that held that responsibility.

Imam Hussain's rise – which culminated in the tragedy of Karbala – was due to the specific circumstances that he faced. Reasons specific to the time made revolution incumbent upon him. These specific circumstances and reasons were not present for the other Imams. Their immaculate nature demanded that each of them perform his obligation based on the conditions of the time. Each had a designated assignment in accordance to the divine plan.

This should be clear. However, here we are attempting to understand – to the extent we can –the specific conditions that were characteristic of the time of Imam Hussain's movement that compelled him to rise. If we contemplate on what we mentioned in the previous chapters, the uniqueness of the circumstances facing Imam Hussain should be clear. But it will also be beneficial to detail the distinctions between his circumstances and those of the other Imams.

## IMAM ALI'S CONCERNS

After disruption of the divine mandate – the deviation of the Muslim nation's system of governance – it seems that the Commander of the Faithful was concerned with two important matters critical to preserving and sustaining the faith.

*Preserving the Message*

The Commander of the Faithful preserved the general structure of Islam that the Prophet and his righteous companions worked tirelessly to erect. The teachings of Islam had to be protected. They had to be spread amongst a large group of individuals that will carry and defend them. Even if those people were to defend the faith for their personal interests and privileges, the message had to be protected. It is narrated that God will support his religion with malevolent individuals, despite their malicious intentions.[1]

All of this is in order to spread the message of Islam to the distant nations – so they can receive wisdom, learn the truth, and find guidance. Despite the negatives caused by deviations from the divine message, entering within Islam's general structure is a key to knowing the original Islam and the righteous sect after exploring the differences amongst the Muslims.

However, if the general structure of Islam collapses, it will preclude these nations from being exposed to the true message of the faith. This remains true even if the faction that ascribes to the true tenets of the faith is a minority over-

---

[1] Al-Tousi, *al-Tahtheeb*, 6:134.

powered in numbers and resources by the powerful majority that aims to distort Islam.

## Preserving Life

Imam Ali also had the duty of preserving his own life and the lives of his most loyal and devoted companions. He was ready to make any sacrifice so long as he and his dedicated followers could carry the message unaltered and undistorted.

But they had to wait for their opportunity. When the time was right, they would be able to disseminate their message to the masses.

Imam Ali also had a priority to prepare an elite few that will carry the message of Islam, disseminate it, and rally people around its teachings. This would allow for the message to remain protected from any attempts to extinguish its light or efface its teachings. The sustainability of the true message of Islam will preclude the altered version of Islam from monopolizing the world.

## PRESERVING THE FAITH

This makes it clear why the Commander of the Faithful did not have the platform to offer the same sacrifice as Imam Hussain. We can list the reasons as follows.

Firstly, a head-on conflict following the departure of the Prophet would have resulted in the disintegration and weakening of the religion. The religion of Islam would have entirely collapsed. At the time, many Muslims were still new to the faith and did not have a solid attachment to it or a clear understanding of its tenets. A serious conflict might cause them to react and reject the faith. This is very different than the time of Imam Hussain where Islam was more established, widely spread, and more integrated in its followers' lives. All of that was due to the moral and monetary benefits that its followers garnered.

If we analyze that period of history, we will see that the rise of a dominant and geographically vast nation in the name of Islam is one of the most critical factors that contributed to the preservation of the faith. The conquests of the early caliphs struck awe in the hearts of many. The spoils of war had enriched tribal leaders and war-chiefs. Since Islam was successfully exploited to create such a powerful state, many in this elite class saw it in their interest to preserve the faith in order to preserve their source of power and revenue.

Secondly, a head-on conflict will endanger the lives of Imam Ali and his handful of righteous followers. If they were to be eliminated, there will be no advocate for the true message of Islam. There will be a vacuum that the tyrannical state will fill. The state's version of Islam – altered and contaminated – will spread without opposition.

Yet the sacrifices of the Commander of the Faithful and his companions are not clear to the masses – definitely not as clear as the sacrifice of Imam Hussain. This is due to a number of reasons. During Imam Ali's era, the principles of Islam were still not engrained in the hearts and minds of ordinary Muslims. The status and significance of the Progeny and their oppression was not as apparent to people. Thus, most viewed the conflict as a struggle for political power.

Conversely, the circumstances are tremendously different with Imam Hussain. People started to better understand and appreciate the divine status of the Progeny and the oppression they had endured. This change was due to the tireless efforts of Imam Hussain's immaculate predecessors – Imam Ali, Lady Fatima, and Imam Hassan – and their companions. Their efforts set the stage for Imam Hussain's movement.

During this period, the features of the call to Shia Islam became clear and apparent. There was a large audience ready to receive its teachings. People were ready to resort in their faith to the Prophet's Household. The tragedy of Karbala was a turning point for Islam. It elevated the faith and became an integral catalyst behind its strength, growth, and popularity with the masses.

## READJUSTING THE COURSE OF HISTORY

Imam Ali did attempt to rise in the face of deviation. But it was imperative that his movement does not culminate in the most terrible of tragedies – that was the fate of Imam Hussain. Rather, the drive of his movement was to fix the course of Islam by recruiting a righteous group of devout followers. Their mission would be to preserving the faith by upholding its sacred tenets. Their very presence would deter deviants from their attempts to exploit the religion of Islam.

However, as the Muslim traditions mention that the Imam did not find enough victors to pursue his strategy.[2]

---

[2] This was partially discussed in the book *Fi Rihab Al-Aqeeda* by his Eminence Grand Ayatollah Muhammad Saeed Al-Hakeem.

Thus, Imam Ali was forced to remain silent, exercise patience, and preserve his life and the lives of the righteous few that remained steadfast with him. They awaited the appropriate opportunity to exercise their role in curbing deviance. They would wait until the opportunity arose to reveal the truth and warn the people about the dismal path that the nation was taking.

## Passing on the Opportunity?

Some claim that deviation occurred because the Commander of the Faithful was not firm in responding to the deviators. He did not want to react before events unfolded and was occupied in the Prophet's burial. In those circumstances, others took advantage and took over.

The proponents of this claim concede that the Imam was able to preserve his principles and values in a manner that is truly admirable. He exemplified the greatest level of respect and reverence for the Prophet. The Imam said, "Would I leave the Messenger of God unburied in his home while I go out to compete for his authority?" He also wanted to demonstrate to the people that political authority is not a prize for people to compete for. It is a right that the Muslims must deliver to him and is forbidden for anyone else.

However, these claimants allege that, with this approach, he provided the opportunity for the deviants to usurp the right of the Muslims in having a just leader. Avoiding this outcome, they claim, is more important than preserving the principles and values above.

This claim is clearly erroneous.

It is narrated through various channels that the Prophet instructed Imam Ali with respect to this matter and the Imam would not violate these instructions.

The Imam is narrated to have said,

> The Messenger of God told me, 'if they gather against you, do what I have commanded you. Stay your chest to the ground.'[3] When they deviated away from me, I [persevered] despite the adversity. I closed my eyelids and endured the pricking in my eyes. I stayed my chest to the ground...[4]

There are a number of possible interpretations for this saying.

In its early stages, the esteemed call of Islam did not settle in and hold a sacred presence in the souls of the believers. If Imam Ali – who represents the Prophet – displayed an interest in pursuing power while leaving the Prophet's body unattended to, this would have negatively reflected on the sacred nature of the faith and its principles. It would have irreversibly weakened the call of Islam in the psyche of the believers. This would have been a great danger perceived by the Imam.

In His absolute knowledge, God knows that even if Imam Ali raced to attain power, his bid would have ultimately been unsuccessful. Quraysh was determined to usurp the caliphate from the Holy Household generally and Imam Ali specifically. They were willing to do whatever it took to achieve this desire. In addition, Imam Ali did not have

---

[3] 'Stay your chest to the ground' is an Arabic expression meaning 'do not react.' –Eds.

[4] Al-Mutazili, *Sharh Nahj Al-Balagha*, 20:326.

enough supporters who were committed and devoted to the truth that he could have mobilized to stand against the usurpers.

For Imam Ali to successfully hold on to his right, an internal conflict would have had to ensue between the *Muhajiroon* and the *Ansar*. This internal strife would have weakened Islam and resulted in widespread uproar by the Muslims who were still lacking in their newly acquired faith. Few followers of the true teachings of Islam would survive the struggle; they would be too few and too weak to be able to preserve and strengthen the faith. Thus, such a conflict in the formative years of Islam, directly after the passing of the Prophet, would have posed an existential threat to the religion and its followers.

So let us suppose, as a hypothetical, that Imam Ali had preempted his adversaries and sought allegiance before they could garner enough supporters. What would the result have been? Certainly, they would have remained adamant in pursuit of their goal.

In fact, Imam Ali and his righteous supporters could have been eliminated as a result of the aforementioned conflict. If that were to happen, the faith would be completely altered and distorted. There would be no one to deliver the original and pure message to the people, leaving a vacuum for the deviants to occupy.

And what if, hypothetically, Imam Ali was to give in to their demands after he had attempted to preempt the coup? That would be even more detrimental to his stature and position. Giving in to their demands would have been seen as a grant of legitimacy to their bid.

Additionally, if the usurpers felt threatened by Imam Ali in any way, they would have killed him as they did with Saad ibn Ubada, the Ansar's candidate for political leadership. In fact, it is narrated that they did attempt to assassinate Imam Ali even though he did not compete with them – after all, he was the rightful successor and he delayed his allegiance to the first caliph.

If this is the case, we can only imagine how events would have unfolded if Imam Ali would have competed for the caliphate and then it was forcefully usurped from him.

## EVALUATING THE SITUATION

Imam Ali's words support this conclusion. Someone once told him,

> O Commander of the Faithful, if the Messenger of God left a young man who had just reached adolescence and the Prophet was comfortable with his maturity; would the Arabs have granted him authority over them?

The Imam replied,

> No. Rather, they would have killed him if he did not do what I did. The Arabs hated the authority of [the Holy Prophet] Muhammad and envied him for the blessings God had bestowed him. His days became too long for them, so they slandered his wife. His she-camel[5] repelled him despite his great kindness towards it and the plentiful bounties he offered it.

---

[5] The Imam uses the she-camel here as a metaphor for the Muslim nation. –Eds.

*The Arabs reached a consensus, during his life, to divert authority away from his Household after his passing. If Quraysh did not take advantage of his name as a justification to rise to power and as a ladder to honor and authority, they would not have worshipped God after his death for one day. They would have reverted into their burrow...*

*Then God opened the doors of conquest [for the nation]. It became affluent after destitution. It became wealthy after strife and hunger. Thus, they began to adore [the command of] Islam after having abhorred it. Faith began to take root in hearts where it was previously unstable. They would say, 'If it [i.e. Islam] was not the truth, this would not happen so.'*

*These conquests were attributed to the designs of the governors and the proficient planning of their generals. People became assured of the astuteness of a group and the quiescence of others.*

*We were of the ones whose mentioning was muffled, whose flame was doused, and whose voice and stature were terminated... Years and eras passed. Many of those who knew passed away. Many of those who did not know were born...*[6]

In assessing the Muslims after the Prophet's departure and the tragic events that transpired, we find them to be weak and fragile – incapable of preserving the integrity of the faith against the conspiracy of Quraysh. It could have been the result of fear or an unrooted faith. The Muslims were indifferent, careless, and treacherous.

---

[6] Al-Mutazili, *Sharh Nahj Al-Balagha*, 20:299.

Imam Ali was forced to deal with them the way he did. He limited his activities to preserving enough of the faith and the faithful in order to counter deviation when the opportunity was ripe.

Praise be to the One that no other like Him is praised for adversity. He has control over all affairs; what has passed and what is to come. Surely, everything goes back to Him.

# IMAM HASSAN'S LEGACY

As we discussed above, Islam was weak during the years directly following the passing of the Holy Prophet – it was still a very young religion and people were still in the process of replacing the corrupt habits of the Age of Ignorance – and a major conflict could have posed an existential threat to its survival. However, this was no longer the case during the time of Imam Hassan. Islam had taken root and succeeding generations were brought up and raised based on its teachings. All the while, Islam continued to grow geographically and the great conquests brought many riches to the Muslim nation. Thus, people became attached to the religion, either because of a firmly held belief, because of social factors and pressures, or simply in aspiration for some material gain.

After the assassination of Imam Ali, Imam Hassan succeeded him as both the carrier of the true teachings of Islam and the head of the Muslim state. By that time, Islam was no longer in its formative stage where a direct confrontation between those who carried Islam's true teachings and those who sought to distort it posed an existential threat to the faith. Thus, the conditions that drove Imam Ali to avoid confrontation directly after the passing of the Prophet were no longer there after the assassination of Imam Ali. Why then did Imam Hassan choose to sign his peace accord with Muawiya, thus putting an end to the current armed confrontation between the Alid and Umayyad lines?

Our analysis leads us to conclude that Imam Hassan made his choice based on the circumstances he faced. These circumstances were wholly different from what Imam Ali faced, and thus require further analysis in order for us to better understand the basis of Imam Hassan's actions and positions.

The discussion of Imam Hassan's legacy will revolve around two major points. First, we will provide a comprehensive overview of his bitter accord with Muawiya. Second, we will discuss his patience and resolute stance even after the betrayal of Muawiya.

## IMAM HASSAN'S ACCORD

There are numerous discussions regarding the accord, some lauding Imam Hassan's position and others disparaging it. For brevity's sake, we will not discuss and comment on all these views. We will simply present and explain our opinion in this regard.

### Impossibility of Military Triumph

Imam Hassan insisted on fighting and defeating Muawiya to preserve the true and pure teachings of the religion of Islam. Yet considering the circumstances of the conflict between the Imam and Muawiya, he would be incapable of succeeding militarily.

Muawiya was becoming stronger and more brutal. The people of Iraq were weak. They felt hopeless and defeated by the government. They were especially weakened by the instigation of the Kharijites, where their ranks divided. Under the tenure of Imam Ali, they had endured five years of civil war. They grew weary and lethargic.

Furthermore, many people lost their faith and some fell to the temptations and lures of Muawiya. They couldn't expect monetary compensation from Imam Hassan, because they knew he followed the same principled path as his father.[1]

Imam Hassan gave the army a choice between making a stance for the sake of the truth, or preserving their lives by making peace. He said,

> Indeed, Muawiya has called us on to a matter that has no glory or justice. If you wish death, we will reject this matter to him and try him to God by the edge of the sword. And if you wish to live, we will accept [his overtures] ...

"Preservation! Preservation!" That was the chant of the overwhelming majority of his army. They made their decision. Left without a supporter, he proceeded with the accord.[2]

---

[1] Please refer to the author's discussion on spoils of war and the clarifications of rules of engagement by Imam Ali detailed in previous chapters. –Eds.

[2] Ibn Al-Atheer, *Usud Al-Ghaba*, 2:13. The reader should keep in mind the provisions of this accord as we proceed in this discussion. The treaty had five provisions:

1. that Muawiya would take political power on the condition that he would act in accordance with the Holy Quran, the tradition of the Prophet, and the model of the righteous caliphs;

2. that Muawiya will not assign an heir to his position, and that after Muawiya's death political power will be transferred to

Imam Hassan had a select group of enlightened supporters in his camp who were determined to proceed with war. But even they did not fully comprehend the circumstances that surrounded them and the reasons for which Imam Hassan signed the accord. When the Imam announced his intentions to enter into the accord with Muawiya, some of them expressed their dissatisfaction with the Imam's position. Despite their devotion, these individuals had a powerful attachment to their rights and rejected Muawiya's falsehoods and oppression. They lost their objectivity in evaluating the situation and assessing the strength of the two sides. They became shortsighted and did not see the long term strategic vision of the Imam.

Imam Hassan clarified this in his speech to his companions narrated by ibn Duraid,

> *Surely by God, we did not avert [battling] the people of the Levant due to any doubt or regret. We used to engage the people of the Levant in battle with comradery and fortitude. Yet comradery has been displaced by enmity, and fortitude has been displaced by despair.*

---

Imam Hassan (or to his brother Imam Hussain in the case that Imam Hassan predeceased Muawiya);

3. that Imam Hassan would not be obliged to call Muawiya "Commander of the Faithful" and that Muawiya would undo the systematic cursing of Imam Ali throughout the territories of the state;

4. peace and security will be allotted to everyone within the territories of the state – whether Arab or non-Arab – and especially to the Shia of Imam Ali and their families; and

5. that the treasury of Kufa is left there and not taken to Damascus and that an allowance is provided for the orphans of those who died in battle on the side of Imam Ali in the battles of the Camel and Siffin.

See: Ibn Katheer, *Al-Bidaya wa Al-Nihaya*, 8:41. –Eds.

*You were alongside your commander in Siffin and your faith was a priority over worldly gains. But now, you have prioritized your worldly gains over your faith.*

*Surely, we are to you the same as we always were. But you are not the same as you had been to us...*

## The Danger of Military Defeat

Imam Hassan saw it better to walk away from the conflict with an agreement founded on certain conditions, rather than a military defeat that would leave Muawiya as the sole authoritative power in the nation.

### Preserving the Shia

Military defeat would have certainly taken an unrecoverable toll on the followers of the Progeny. The closest companions and most dedicated followers of Imam Ali and Imam Hassan would be the first to meet their end. These courageous and loyal companions would always be at the forefront of the battlefield, ready to make the stance and endure the sacrifice. As such, they would be the first victims of a military campaign that is doomed for defeat.

Shia Islam was in dire need of these personalities. They were the ones tasked with carrying the message and propagating it. The Shia had only recently surfaced in the Islamic culture. These insightful and devoted followers were the stronghold of the school of thought of the Progeny. When Imam Ali assumed power, the rights and status of the Progeny were not yet established ideologically amongst the public. Thus, these tenets of Islam did not hold their proper status with the Muslims and remained fickle after the abatement of the authority of the Holy Household.

At that point, Shia Islam became an easy target for Muawiya to wipe out. He was able to triumph and strengthen his empire. However, he did not succeed in wiping out the call of devotion to the Progeny because this righteous group stood firm and steadfast to curtail his ambitions.

These conditions are drastically different than those surrounding Imam Hussain's movement. At the time of Imam Hussain, the message was grounded ideologically and was rooted in the Islamic culture. Thus, the sacrifice of the Imam and his righteous companions did not impact the direction of the faith. In fact, it was a turning point that furnished it with more honor, glory, strength, and stability.

Muawiya breached every condition set out in the accord. He continued his policies of killing, torturing, imprisoning, and displacing many of the Shia. Yet he was not successful in completely eradicating them for the following reasons.

Firstly, Muawiya was not physically able to target and eliminate all of the Shia. When one Shia was killed only more would be born. Many remained and dedicated their efforts to propagate the message during and after his life.

Secondly, even with the Shia he killed, he eliminated them after they had the opportunity to teach and disseminate the message and instill it in society. This preserved the message and allowed it to grow and reach to a broader base within the nation.

Thirdly, the injustices faced by Muawiya's victims and their unwavering commitment to their principles became an insignia of honor for Shia Islam. Shia Islam became a symbol of justice, a call against oppression, and a voice against tyrants. It became the embodiment of sacrifice for the truth.

These injustices and oppressions became a trademark of dishonor for the Umayyad regime. It tainted their reputation and challenged their legitimacy, especially because it reminded people of the Umayyad clan's opposition to the Prophet during the advent of the Message.

Many of the victims of Umayyad tyranny had a commendable impact in Islam and left an honorable legacy with the Muslims. The murder of Hijr ibn Adi and his companions rocked the Muslim nation. This was only one of Muawiya's criminal undertakings. How would the nation view this tyrant when they saw his criminality unfold before their eyes?

**Averting War**

Killing the Shia during war certainly would not have riled the nation. After all, the death of combatants was a natural consequence of war, and not a crime committed by either side. Furthermore, the execution of criminals of war was generally accepted during that time. Thus, capturing and executing Shia combatants would not have been a shock either. Consequently, the Prophet's pardon to his adversaries after the conquest of Mecca and Imam Ali's amnesty to the soldiers after the Battle of the Camel were viewed as great acts of magnanimity.

However, the murder of Imam Hassan, his family members, and his loyal devotees – after the promises and treaties that were in place – would have been regarded as one of the greatest humanitarian crimes by the Muslims universally.

Through the conditions of the accord, Imam Hassan was able to successfully preserve the blood of his followers, who would in turn help protect the teachings of the faith. At the same time, he set the stage for the unmasking of the Umayyad clan, who had killed and persecuted these individuals and others. With every crime to come, the Umayyad clan would be condemned religiously and socially. It was Imam Hassan's work and effort that began to reveal the true colors of these tyrants, resulting in their alienation and condemnation. This was one of the most important achievements in the ongoing struggle to preserve the faith.

## Propaganda

Muawiya was not as arrogant and reckless as Yazid. On the contrary, he had a long-term plan and mission. This seems to have precluded him from rushing to kill Imam Hassan and his family members outside of battle. Their esteemed religious status and their special presence in the souls of the Muslims prevented him from massacring them in the way he had done with others. In fact, he feigned deference to and care for them in order to appear as the forgiving ruler who pardoned his adversaries.

This was an additional challenge for Imam Hassan and his followers. Muawiya's façade of deference and care hindered their ability to effectively propagate their message. They were limited in the extent they could condemn Muawiya's crimes against the faith and the Muslims. The public was conditioned to see grievances against Muawiya as mere soreness and ingratitude expressed by a losing minority.

Muawiya knew this very well and took full advantage of it. He mobilized his media and propaganda machines to mischaracterize the Imam and his followers and tarnish their reputations.

## The Imams and the Accord

Imam Hassan and the other Imams referred to much of what we discussed in explaining their position with respect to Muawiya. In a discussion by Imam Hassan regarding his accord with Muawiya, he said,

> *I have not surrendered a thing to him but for the lack of victors. If I had found [adequate] supporters, I would have fought him day and night until God adjudicates between him and me. However, I have known the people of Kufa and their troubles. Their corrupt are no good for me. They do not have any sense of loyalty and do not fulfill their promises – words and actions. They are hypocrites, for they pronounce that their hearts are with us, but their swords are raised against us...[3]*

In another narration he said, *"I have entered into a truce to avoid bloodshed and out of consideration for myself, my family, and my dedicated companions."* [4]

He also informed Hijr ibn Adi,

> *O Hijr! I have heard your words in the council of Muawiya. Not every person likes what you like and views things like you do. I have not done what I have done but to safeguard you [i.e. the Shia]. And God the Almighty is everyday engaged in a different matter.[5]*

---

[3] Al-Tabrasi, *Al-Ihtijaj*, 2:12.
[4] Ibn Shahrashoob, *Manaqib Aal Abu Talib*, 3:196.
[5] Ibn A'tham, *Al-Futuh*, 4:295*Abu* .

Through this accord, Imam Hassan gave the Shia of the time a new dimension. He transformed them from soldiers in a failing war – condemned by the norms of their time – to a political opposition that was protected by a publically recognized and documented treaty. The regime would be accountable for their protection and the public knew that.

Therefore, they had the right to engage in any activities that served the path of the Progeny. And they fully utilized this opportunity. They offered, for the sake of God, incredible efforts that contributed to the dissemination of the true and pure teachings of the faith amongst the Muslims.

This was especially effectuated when Imam Hassan and his Hashemite aides were able to dedicate the remainder of their lives to spreading true knowledge of Islam. They continued where Imam Ali left off, emphasizing and solidifying the principles he had taught the nation.

Still, Muawiya deprived the Shia of their complete rights and tortured them. He attempted to eradicate them and limit their ability in spreading the call to the Progeny. However, this only served to strengthen the path of Progeny. It became a reason for crystallizing and revealing the message and disseminating it throughout the nation.

### Until the Last Breath?

With everything we discussed, there is no room left for one to say that 'it was imperative for Imam Hassan to continue with war – not in order to triumph, as that was impossible under the circumstances, but to battle until the last breath and to sacrifice his life and the lives of his household like Imam Hussain did.'

This is a clearly an immature and confused argument.

Imam Hussain's sacrifice was not undertaken out of pride. It was not simply to reject oppression and forbid evil – Imam Hassan would have shared in that.

Rather, it was a necessary sacrifice, considering the circumstances of his time, within a long-term vision. The achievements of Imam Hussain would not have been possible during the time of Imam Hassan. The circumstances and conditions at his time were different than those of Imam Hussain.

First, Muawiya seized the caliphate after a grinding war he justified by calling for vengeance for the blood of Othman. Following that, he took advantage of the event of *Tahkeem*[6] that injected his caliphate with superficial legitimacy. Furthermore, his persistence in conflict and an expanding military base made him a near invincible force that had to be dealt with differently.

He was not like Yazid who seized power as an heir to the throne similar to the Roman and Persian dynasties. The

---

[6] *Tahkeem* – literally, 'the arbitration' – was an arbitration between two delegates from the two warring sides that had met at the Battle of Siffin. Muawiya chose Amr ibn Al-Aas as his delegate. Ali ibn Abu Talib wished to appoint one of his close companions, but mutiny in his camp pressured him to send Abu Musa Al-Ashari as the delegate. Ibn Al-Aas and Al-Ashari met for the arbitration and, after a long negotiation, came to a conclusion – that both Ali ibn Abu Talib and Muawiya should be removed from power and that the Muslims should be free to choose a new leader. Al-Ashari got on the pulpit, announced this decision, and called ibn Al-Aas to confirm the decision. However, when ibn Al-Aas got on the pulpit, he declared that they have agreed to remove Ali ibn Abu Talib and that Muawiya is the rightful ruler. The trickery of ibn Al-Aas was evident to all who were present and the arbitration served only to inflame the civil war rather than end it. See: Al-Mutazili, *Sharh Nahj Al-Balagha*, 2:256. –Eds.

Muslim nation initially condemned such a hereditary system. Moreover, Yazid did not impose his power as a force on the ground like Muawiya did. Thus, Yazid lacked the same sense of legitimacy that his father had possessed.

The mere fact that the Imam knew of Muawiya's illegitimacy did not impose an obligation on him to rise, especially since his position was not supported by general sentiments throughout the nation.

Second, Imam Hassan's stance could easily be painted as engrossment in a power struggle. To the Muslim public, he had a claim to legitimate political authority after being given allegiance by the people of Kufa. For the devoted followers of the Progeny, his right was God-given and undisputable. Thus, he legitimately held the reins of power, at least in Kufa. An armed stance would simply be seen as an effort to expand the geographic area he controlled.

This was not the case with Imam Hussain, who had simply rejected to pay allegiance to someone like Yazid. He did not leave Medina to seek political power, as was obvious in his movement. Rather, battle was imposed on him by the army of Yazid.

In other words, people would have seen Imam Hassan's stance as engrossment in a losing battle driven either by reactionary zeal or a stubborn mentality. Conversely, Imam Hussain was in a position of self-defense in an oppressive battle that attempted to force him to pay an oath of allegiance that he rejected and was not obliged by.

Third, as was mentioned previously, Muawiya was not reckless and indifferent like Yazid. Unlike Yazid, he did not commit the same atrocious crimes that elevated to the level of the terrible tragedy of Karbala. It was likely that Muawiya would spare Imam Hassan and his family members after eliminating all of his supporters – a disastrous outcome, as discussed previously.

Fourth, in the eyes of the Muslims, the long and bitter tenure of the Umayyad rule under Muawiya provided more justifications for Imam Hussain to challenge the Umayyad regime. During the time of Imam Hassan, the nation had yet to endure enough Umayyad atrocities in order to come to this conclusion. Imam Hassan's patience and sacrifices throughout this period allowed for the Muslims to see this reality.

Fifth, the level of corruption and disregard to the faith was much more visible publically during Yazid's era than Muawiya's. While Muawiya did a better job at concealing the institutional corruption he led, Yazid's bold disregard for decency and open corruption was undeniable.

There are many other reasons that a contemplator can reflect on to further understand the drastic differences in the circumstances and conditions between the eras of Imam Hassan and Imam Hussain. Their different circumstances imposed different obligations for each in fulfilling their ultimate goal of preserving the faith and its followers.

**An Immaculate Stance**

We find that Imam Hussain supported Imam Hassan's position. He continued with the same mission and retained the status quo with Muawiya for ten years following the death of Imam Hassan.

When Imam Hussain refused to comply with Muawiya's request to pay allegiance to Yazid, and this became known in the public domain, the Shia aspired to uproot Muawiya. Ju'da ibn Hubayra wrote to Imam Hussain from Kufa,

> *Your Shia look up to you and do not equate anyone with you. They saw your brother, [Imam] Hassan's position in avoiding war. They know you to be kind with your followers, stern with your enemies, and firm in God's way. If you desire this matter, come to us. We have dedicated ourselves to die with you.*

Imam Hussain answered him in a letter that he publicized to all the people of Kufa, where he explains,

> *As for my brother, I pray that God has blessed him and supported him [in the hereafter]. As for me, I do not see that the day has come. Stand your ground, may God have mercy on you. Remain in your homes. Take caution against the suspicions [of the Umayyad state] so long as Muawiya remains alive....[7]*

An objective examination of Imam Hassan's circumstances demonstrates the greatness of his courageous stance in serving the faith. It displays his complete sacrifice for the sake of the religion. Through his stance, he swallowed the pain and agony inflicted on him by the Umayyads. Additionally, he was subject to the people's ignorance, which unjustly characterized him as timid and overly concerned with his own life.

---

[7] Abu Hanifa, *Al-Akhbar Al-Tiwal*, 222.

He also endured reproach and criticism from his own followers, who were shortsighted and ignorant of the wisdom in his actions.

By exercising patience and enduring the melees for the sake of preserving the religion, Imam Hassan ascended to the greatest heights of struggling in the way of God and sacrificing for Him. To God we belong and to Him we shall return.

## NON-CONFRONTATION

From day one, Muawiya expressed his unwillingness to adhere to the terms of the accord. When he entered Kufa, he proclaimed, "Everything I gave Hassan ibn Ali is beneath my feet. I shall not fulfill my promise."

Despite the fact that Muawiya's breach justifies Imam Hassan in abandoning the accord, the previous conditions and obstacles did not change in his favor such that he could rescind the agreement and declare war.

Indeed, conditions could have deteriorated further following the disintegration of the army of the Imam and the comfortable arrival of Muawiya and his military to the outskirts of Kufa. Furthermore, the Imam's companions split as a result of their differing positions with respect to the accord.

Muawiya soon discovered this fragmentation in the Imam's camp and quickly announced his opinion regarding the terms of the agreement. Otherwise, it would be foolish for him to gamble with a hasty announcement unless he realized all the consequences. It was possible that the circumstances would have shifted in favor of Imam Hassan, but that would have taken a great deal of time.

Time would ensure the settling and establishment of the Shia creed amongst the followers and the nation at large. The Imam wanted to ensure it was strong enough before the righteous few of the Shia sacrificed themselves with Imam Hussain.

Time could also show the true colors of the Umayyad regime. Muawiya recklessly disregarded the pure principles of Islam and the rights of the Muslims. His rescinding of the agreement became more visible publically, as well as his persecution of the Progeny and their devotees.

*The movement of the Shia during the life of Imam Hassan*

Perhaps it was Muawiya's blatant disregard for the treaty that drove a group of Shia in Kufa to return to Imam Hassan and request from him to confront Muawiya. It is reported that one delegation came to him and said,

> *Our astonishment for your treaty with Muawiya never fades. You had an army of forty thousand Kufans, all in your payroll and all ready to protect their homes. A similar number of their sons and followers were also ready. They all gathered, except for your followers in Basra and Hijaz. But you did not take any guarantee that you will be treated well, nor did you take any wealth from the treasury. After having done what you did, why did you not make the notables of east and west as witnesses and guarantors for the deal against Muawiya? Why don't you write to him demanding that authority is relinquished to you after his death? This would make circumstances much easier for us. Instead, you*

*chose to make a deal between the two of you, but he did not keep his end of the bargain. He did not hesitate to proclaim to all people, 'I had agreed to conditions and made promises only to douse the flames of war and to end sedition. Now that God has united us, our word and affinity, and protected us from division, all that is now under my feet.' By God, I would have risen against him after that if it was not for your treaty with him. But now he has breached [the accord]. If you would like, let us prepare for a short war. Declare your march towards Kufa. Remove his governor there and declare his loss of authority. You would have replied to their violation of the treaty. Surely, God does not like the traitors.*

Imam Hassan replied to them,

*You are our followers and admirers. You know that if I were working to achieve worldly goals, or if I were to work and scheme to gain power, I would be no less powerful, generous, or resolute than Muawiya. But I am of a different opinion than yours. I did not do what I did for any reason other than averting bloodshed. So accept God's judgment and submit to Him. Remain at home. Refrain [from revolution]. Sheathe your blades...[8]*

Even though there were slight improvements in the overall situation, Imam Hassan did not elect to disregard the accord and go back to war. In fact, the situation deteriorated further in at least two ways.

---

[8] Al-Balathiri, *Ansab Al-Ashraaf*, 3:290-91.

**First: Muawiya Strengthened his Authority During his Governance**

Muawiya disregarded the principles of the faith and transgressed against the rights of the Muslims. He bought the consciences of many who were well off. He bolstered his authority and strengthened his power using extortion and bribery. Thus, there was no group of righteous individuals who were truly ready to answer the call of Imam Hassan – unlike those who answered the call of Imam Hussain, even though they eventually betrayed him or failed to support him.

**Second: Muawiya's Exploitation of the Accord**

Imam Hassan was restricted by an accord with Muawiya that prohibited him from confronting him militarily.

Muawiya's breach of the terms was a legitimate religious and practical justification for Imam Hassan to abandon the accord. However, Muawiya, possessing powerful media and propagation forces, would have been able to fool the general public and portray Imam Hassan as an antagonist who transgressed. With this, Muawiya would weaken the morale of the Imam's followers and would tarnish his image. The message that the Imam was responsible to protect and uphold would be disastrously harmed if this were to happen.

In other words, the Imam was obligated to protect the faith, not simply by preserving its religious symbols, but also by distancing himself from suspicion. He would need to avoid anything that could be utilized by the enemies to tarnish his reputation – even if it was built on falsehood, deception, and lies.

It is narrated from the Prophet that when his companions requested from him to kill Abdullah ibn Ubay – after he announced his hostile position towards the message of Islam and the Prophet – he said, "People should not [be given an excuse to] say that Muhammad kills his companions."[9]

This is a typical propaganda method that the wicked utilize in slandering their adversaries. Muawiya himself had written a letter to Imam Hussain and said,

> *I have heard some things about you. I hope that they are not true, as I expect more from you. By God, whoever is given the trust and oath of God must be worthy of fulfilling it. The most trustworthy in fulfilling their oaths are men like you, who hold high stature, nobility, and God-given status. So take care of yourself. Fulfill the oath of God. But if you reject me, I will reject you. And if you plot against me, I will plot against you. So be wary that you do not cause disunity in this nation.[10]*

In his letter, Muawiya overlooks the fact that he was the first one to breach the accord. Thus, Imam Hussain answered him with a letter in which he highlights the crimes of the Umayyad regime.

> *You have ridden on your ignorance. You have taken great strides to break your covenants. I swear, you have not fulfilled a single covenant. You have breached your oath by murdering these men after promising peace, granting amnesty, and making oaths and guarantees. You did not do this*

---

[9] Al-Nisaburi, *Sahih Muslim*, 8:19.
[10] Al-Daynouri, *Al-Imama wa Al-Siyasa*, 1:188.

*for any reason other than the fact that they recited our vir-*
*tues and praised our position...*[11]

If this is how Muawiya addressed Imam Hussain, we can only imagine how he would address the general public. How perverse would he be in utilizing his propaganda machine to slander the names of Imam Hassan and Imam Hussain?

Therefore, Imam Hassan was not in a position that permitted him to achieve the goal of preserving the faith through a sacrifice like the sacrifice of Imam Hussain. Additionally, he was not able to engage in a conflict with Muawiya to reform and restore the path of the faith, which deviated after the Prophet's passing. The call by a large number of Shia in Kufa for Imam Hassan to rise and reform, after Muawiya breached the accord and mistreated them, originated from a reactionary shortsightedness. They had love for the Progeny and detestation of the Umayyad regime, but lacked understanding of the Progeny's vision and strategy to protect the faith.

## Imam Hussain's Position

We find that the same conditions and obstacles that were present during Imam Hassan's time remained as the status quo when Imam Hussain became the Imam. Because his circumstances were the same, Imam Hussain adopted the same policy as his brother Imam Hassan. When he was asked by the people of Kufa to rise up against Muawiya, he emphasized that he would not rise so long as Muawiya was alive.

---

[11] Ibid, 1:202-08

# THE PROGENY

We have explained that complete and instantaneous reformation and restoration of the faith after its deviance was not possible. All the Imams of the Progeny were aware of this from day one, although they did not have the opportunity to express and emphasize it until the aftermath of the tragedy of Karbala.

The progeny of Imam Hussain had no need to offer a great sacrifice similar to that of Imam Hussain.

As explained earlier, Imam Hussain's sacrifice was not because of a reactionary or temperamental attitude. It was also not motivated by pride, honor, or something of that nature.

Imam Hussain's sacrifice came at the culmination of the reform project initiated by Imam Ali and advanced by the immaculate stance of Imam Hassan. The sacrifice at Karbala achieved the Imams' intended goals – namely, elucidating the pure teachings of the faith, stripping the state of its religious guise, and strengthening the call of Shia Islam within the Muslim nation.

All of this was accomplished with the efforts of the first three Imams and their loyal devotees, which culminated in the greatest sacrifice in the tragedy of Karbala.

After all this, there was no need for the later Imams and their Shia to offer a similar sacrifice. Following the tragedy of Karbala, the door for opposing, exposing, and revealing the crimes of the governing regime opened up. Many factions in society, even non-Shia, realized and understood the illegitimacy of the government and started to rise against it.

## PRESERVING THE SHIA

The Imams urged the Shia to preserve their lives and safeguard their blood. They instructed their followers to not confront the ruler or express their opposition to the state. The Shia were instructed to avoid controversy and disputes with the masses, and to distance themselves from fame and publicity in order to avoid being targets of public mockery.

Thus, the Imams emphasized *taqiyya* and patience in enduring the hardships imposed by their enemies. We see these instructions in countless traditions that cannot be encompassed here. One can find these decrees with minimal research into their sublime heritage and analysis of their practices.

Consequently, the Imams were successful in braking the accumulated rage and anger of the Shia and limiting their emotional reactions. They had to preserve their lives.

## STRENGTHENING THE BASE

The next stage for the Imams – by the commandments and support of God and His Messenger – was to strengthen the Shia base, elucidate the teachings of Islam, and invest in the accumulated gains of their immaculate predecessors. Ultimately, their goal was the same as their predecessors – they are the guardians of the faith and are tasked with its preservation.

The Imams from the progeny of Imam Hussain endured a set of circumstances different from those of their predecessors. As such, their charge was to emphasize the following points.

### A Practical Truce

The Imams were able to show the Shia that under the present circumstances, establishing the full extent of true divine leadership and pursuing total reform of the nation are impracticable goals. Consequently, the Imams and their followers entered into a truce with the oppressive government until the rise of the Twelfth Holy Imam. Nonetheless, even with such a truce, the Imams stressed the importance of not becoming heedless of the oppression of the government and its illegitimacy. Moreover, there was an obligation in exposing the regime and a prohibition on cooperating with it. This demonstrates that there was a clear divide between the followers of the Imams and the oppressive rulers of the nation.

This truce with the government rendered a number of significant gains for the Imams and their devoted followers.

The Imams wanted to avoid setting up the Shia for failure by expending their talents, capabilities, and energy on useless or counterproductive efforts. They desired for them to employ their capabilities in advancing their lives and faith. In fact, stepping outside of the political sphere will naturally allow for the Shia to focus their attention on their religious affairs. They will be able to express their repressed faith, solidify their identity, and establish their base. This was a silent stance against the successive tyrannical dynasties that came to power.

Despite their opposition to the regime, the Shia were allowed a certain degree of freedom. The state was preoccupied with the armed oppositions that continued to prop up every now and then. The Shia's silent and nonviolent stance did not pose as imminent of a threat as these armed oppositions. Thus, the Shia were not always at the government's crosshairs. This did not only strengthen Shia Islam, but also drew sympathy for the followers of the Progeny whenever the state carried on its policies of persecution.

*Focusing on the Oppression of the Progeny*

There was a distinct focus on the tragedy of Karbala – specifically on the emotional facet of the event. There was an effort to remind people of the oppression and injustices endured by the Progeny and the repression of their message.

The Imams employed the emotional aspects of the tragedy to solidify the Shia identity. The Imams utilized various events and occasions to remind people of the tragedy and allow them to engage with it. They stressed the importance of reviving the remembrance of Imam Hussain by lamenting, reciting poetry, shedding tears, gathering in commemoration of the event, and using other forms of expression. The Imams continued to highlight through various narrations the great rewards that a believer attains through participating in mourning Imam Hussain's tragedy.

Through all of this, the Imams opened the doors for their Shia in two ways that other Muslims did not have due to the repressed circumstances and the difficulties of the time, which distanced people from understanding their faith. First, the Imams emphasized the visitation of Imam Hussain. Second, they ensured that the tragedy would regularly be remembered by establishing its annual anniversary as a time of weeping and sorrow.

There is a primary emphasis on the visitation of Imam Hussain and the visitation of the other Immaculate Imams, their children, and their righteous followers. For brevity's sake, we will highlight one narration that touches on some of the remarkable aspects of the visitation.

It is narrated through various channels that Muawiya ibn Wahab, a companion of Imam al-Sadiq, once visited the Imam and found him in prayer. After completing his prayer, Imam al-Sadiq commenced with the following supplication.

*O God who has privileged us with honor, promised us intercession, bestowed us with authority, granted us knowledge of the past and what is to come, and made the hearts of people flock to us.*

*Forgive me, my brothers, and the visitors of the grave of Abu Abdullah Al-Hussain. They have spent their wealth and expended their efforts in their desire to please us. They hoped to gain [Your rewards] through associating with us. They brought joy to your Prophet. They complied with our command. They angered our enemies. They sought Your satisfaction.*

*So reward them with Your acceptance. Protect them during the night and day. Guard their families and children whom they left behind with the best of Your guardianship. Shield them from the evils of every stubborn tyrant and from every creature of Yours, whether weak or strong. [Shield them from] the evil of the demons of mankind and jinn. Grant them the best of what they hoped to receive from You…*

*So have mercy on the faces that were altered by the sun. Have mercy on the cheeks that roll over on the grave of Abu Abdullah Al-Hussain. Have mercy on the eyes that shed tears out of sympathy for us. Have mercy on the hearts that anguished and burned for us…*[1]

It seems that the Shia – rather, the Muslims in general – had an affinity for this visitation from day one. It is narrated from Imam Zain Al-Abideen that when he returned with the mourning family from the Levant to Medina,[2] they requested from the guide to take them through Karbala. When they arrived to the location where Imam Hussain was massacred, they found Jabir ibn Abdullah Al-Ansari – the Prophet's companion – along with a group of Hashemites and others that came to visit the grave of Imam Hussain.

---

[1] Al-Qummi, *Kamil Al-Ziyarat*, 228-29.

[2] After the massacre at Karbala, the remaining members of the household of the Prophet – mostly women and children – were taken as captives and paraded through some of the major cities in the Muslim nation. They were taken from Karbala, through Kufa, Mosul, and Aleppo, and to Damascus in the Levant, passing by numerous cities and villages on the way. After completing the arduous journey, they were allowed to the city of their grandfather, Medina. –Eds.

They greeted each other with lamentations and tears.[3] It is said that Jabir was the first individual to visit the grave of Imam Hussain.

From day one, the grave of Imam Hussain was meant to become a religious symbol for the devotees of the Prophet's Progeny. As Imam Zain Al-Abideen and the mourning family would look at the slain bodies of their relatives, Lady Zaynab would comfort them and say,

> *Do no despair for what you see. By God, this is a covenant by the Messenger of God to your grandfather, father, and your uncle. God has decreed for a group of people – unknown to the Pharaohs of the time but known by the denizens of the heavens – to collect all these severed limbs and slain bodies and bury them. They will build on this plain a grave for your father, the Master of Martyrs, whose mark will never be effaced...*

Of course, visitation of the grave of Imam Hussain was not the only tradition of mourning and commemoration that the Imams established. It is narrated that Imam Ali Al-Rida would say,

> *My father would never be seen smiling during the month of Muharram. Sorrow would overcome him until the end of the ten days. The tenth day for him was a day of tragedy, grief, and weeping. He would say, 'this is the day when Hussain was killed...'*[4]

The Progeny would continue to ensure that the Shia have an extraordinary attachment to Imam Hussain. His grave is

---

[3] Al-Majlisi, *Bihar Al-Anwar*, 145-46.
[4] Al-Sadouq, *Al-Amaali*, 190.

given special attributes. Under his dome, prayers are answered. The close vicinity around his grave holds a special status similar to the Grand Mosque in Mecca, the Prophet's Mosque in Medina, and the Grand Mosque of Kufa.[5]

There are some who wish the Shia to end their mourning for Imam Hussain. They say, "Imam Hussain was killed for reform, not for us to cry and wail."

If we observe how human society interacts with any reality, we would quickly realize that the memory of such tragedies is quickly forgotten. As years, decades, and centuries pass, so too does the popular conscience of such events. They are merely stories mentioned in books of history, and considered insignificant to a large portion of society.

Thus, if it were not for the persistence of the Shia in reviving the remembrance of the tragedy of Karbala, the resonance of the event would have diminished. People would have forgotten the scenes of that day in the year 61 AH, just like most historical occurrences have been forgotten.

But because of the efforts of the Imams and their devout followers, we see that this tragedy plays an active role in the makeup and identity of the Shia. More than a millennium has passed, and its memory still lingers in the operative memory of the followers of the Progeny.

---

[5] In Shia jurisprudence, four lands are given special status. In those lands, a traveler is given a choice between performing prayers as complete or shortened prayers. These lands are the city of Mecca, the city of Medina, the city of Kufa, and the close vicinity around the grave of Imam Hussain. For more detail, see the many books of jurisprudence that the Shia scholars have authored. –Eds.

The Imams continued to emphasize the depravity of their enemies. They foretold of the fates of those who committed atrocities like the tragedy of Karbala and others. They disavowed them and instructed their followers to do the same.

In addition, the Imams stressed the illegitimacy of the successive tyrannical regimes. They forbade their followers from becoming part of these tyrannical governments and partaking in their criminal activities. Exceptions were made only for cases of necessity or where there is a greater benefit that can be reaped for the advancement of the faith and its followers. These nuances are detailed in the books of jurisprudence.

*God and His Servants*

The Imams focused on the importance of connecting with God and seeking His pleasure. They stressed that followers most believe, commit and devote themselves entirely to God. We are to seek His rewards and fear His displeasure. They guided us by example to be always in a state of remembrance of God. Our thoughts are only positive in His regard, because nothing but good comes from Him. We respond to trials and tribulation with patience and forbearance, drawing our strength from His limitless support. We seek refuge in no one but God, calling onto Him and connecting to His grace for our salvation. Devotion to God and reverence to Him was a known mark of the Shia in the early generations. The Imams sought to ensure that this remains the case for the generations that followed.

They did not only teach their followers the importance of seeking this proximity to God. They embodied it. They were the immaculate guides of the nation. They attained the highest levels of dedication in their faith. They submitted to the will of their Lord. Their impeccable character was, and will always remain, an example for the world to uphold.

Their teachings in this regard are too numerous to mention and too vast to survey. If the reader wishes to learn more about their heritage, the books of history and narrations are plentiful and widespread. The Shia scholars – the guardians of this heritage – have dedicated their lives to understanding and disseminating this knowledge.

But their heritage does not stop at their sayings and traditions that are listed in the books of history and tradition. They utilized supplication and prayer as a distinct venue to disseminate their teachings. The supplications and visitations are unique in their eloquent rhetoric and oratory style. Within their marvelous style, they hold deep and insightful thoughts and ideas. Thus, they touch the hearts and leave a profound imprint on the mind.

Engaging in these rituals and supplications is not particular to the Shia scholars or any one group. On the contrary, the door is wide open for all Shia to participate especially with the presence of many occasions throughout the year. These occasions have become public seasons where massive numbers of people rally around the holy shrines and other significant places of worship. These ongoing rituals became part and parcel of the rich heritage that define the Shia. They continue to grow and flourish despite all the challenges and obstacles.

The Imams also continued to emphasize the importance of the position of divine leadership that they held. They elucidated the true meaning of this leadership and the qualities of anyone who holds such a status. They explained to their devout followers the meaning of their immaculate nature.

Imam Ali Al-Hadi gathered all the scattered information from his forefathers that speak to the lofty stature of the Imams, the obligation to follow them, their oppression, and the necessity to disavow their enemies. He provided the Shia with two comprehensive texts that encompass all these ideas –Al-Ziyara Al-Jami'a Al-Kabeera (the Grand Encompassing Visitation) and Visitation of the Day of Ghadeer.

These two visitations suffice in themselves to present and embody Shia ideology with respect to the status of the Progeny. They stand to remind the Shia and ground them in their creed. As to the other major and minor supplications, prayers, recitations, and spiritual works, they are too many to enumerate and discuss here. The reader is encouraged to refer to the books of prayers and supplications, which are readily accessible and available.

*Reviving the Teachings of the Prophet*

All the efforts of the Imams, in essence, were intended to revive the teachings of the Prophet. They strived to undue the decades of fabrications and distortion at the hands of the government.

The Imams opened the gates of knowledge that they inherited from the Prophet. They are truly the gates to his city of knowledge.[6] They presented the true theological tenets, emphasized philosophical truths, taught the highest codes of ethics, imparted the parables of the prophets, and conveyed

---

[6] The Prophet is narrated to have said, "I am the city of knowledge and Ali is its gate." Al-Nisaburi, *al-Mustadrak*, 5:330. –Eds.

other knowledge that God has distinctly imparted them with.

The Imams from the progeny of Imam Hussain were able to allocate all of their time and effort to embark on this endeavor.

**The Scholars**

The Imams attempted to educate their Shia and impart their culture via their companions, select narrators, and the carriers of their heritage. The Imams assigned these individuals to become agents that can carry and deliver their knowledge and teachings to the Shia.

It is narrated by Hisham ibn Salim that Imam al-Sadiq said,

> When death approached my father, he instructed me, 'O Jafar, I request from you to take care of my companions.' I said, 'May I be your ransom! By God, I will leave them [with such knowledge that] they will not need to ask anyone in any land.'[7]

Thus, the Imams stressed in many narrations for their followers to refer to the scholars and learn from them.

In one narration, someone asks Imam al-Sadiq how a dispute between two individuals should be resolved. The Imam said,

> Look for someone amongst you who narrates our words, has insight into what is permissible and impermissible, and knows our verdicts. They should accept his verdict, for I have given him authority over you. If he rules by our author-

---

[7] Al-Kulayni, *Al-Kafi*, 1:306.

*ity but is refuted, then God's verdict has been belittled and*
*we have been rejected. One who rejects us rejects God...*[8]

Furthermore, in another narration signed by the Twelfth Imam, he reiterates, *"As to your practical matters, refer back to our narrators. They are my proof on you and I am the proof of God..."*[9]

The Imams urged their followers to understand the faith in depth, publish books, teach and learn, and revive their remembrance. The Imams were able during their long tenure with their Shia, despite all the pressures and conflicts, to disseminate their divine teachings and heritage – in creed, jurisprudence, ethics, supplications, visitations, and other areas of knowledge – until it crystallized and settled with their Shia.

**The Seminaries**

A strong and distinct intellectual and cultural presence emerged. The knowledge that the Imams imparted to their Shia created a distinct scholarly community within Islam. For the Shia, this wealth of knowledge was carried and preserved by the seminaries present in different Shia localities.

The Imams sponsored these seminaries for two centuries. They laid out general guidelines and monitored their course until they lined up with the path of the Imams. Consequently, the seminaries distinguished themselves with their meticulous focus on researching and deriving the religious verdicts from their primary sources. They preserved the apparent meanings and precise scope of these sources without

---

[8] Al-Tousi, *Al-Tahtheeb*, 6:218,
[9] Al-Sadouq, *Kamal Al-Deen*, 484.

overreaching with personal speculation or allowing for the infiltration of external influences.

For many centuries and ongoing, the door of religious scholarship and independent reasoning – *ijtihad* – remained open in Shia Islam. For the Shia, *ijtihad* is not tailoring and customizing the religious ruling to be fitting for the changing circumstances and times. It is based on a consistent set of standards anchored by the Prophet and Imams.

The Imams thus set the stage for the Major Occultation of the Twelfth Imam – where the Twelfth Imam ceased direct and open communication with his devotees. Yet the Shia continued and endured. They held on to the wealth of knowledge and wisdom given to them by their immaculate leaders. The implementation of *ijtihad* allowed for successive generations to practice their independent reasoning and discover new depths of meaning within the Holy Quran and the traditions of the Prophet and the Imams.

## The Marjaeya

Due to the dire necessity, especially after the Major Occultation, the *Marjaeya*[10] emerged from the seminaries. Their emergence was in accordance with the religious rulings that God prescribed. There are a number of critical conditions that must be present in a jurist in order for him to be qualified for emulation. One of the essential conditions, after having knowledge of the religious rulings, is that the jurist

---

[10] The Marjaeya – literally 'reference' or 'authority' – is the religious authority that the Shia refer back to and emulate in the matters of their faith. –Eds.

must be just[11] to a degree that is proportional to the weight of the trust that he carries.

In a narration by Imam al-Sadiq, he explains,

> *As to any of the jurists that safeguards himself, preserves his faith, counters his whims, and adheres to the commands his Lord – the public may emulate him.*[12]

The Shia were connected to the Marjaeya in practice, as they referred to it for religious guidance. The Shia were also connected to the Marjaeya emotionally, as they viewed the jurists as the trustees of their faith. People recognized the role of the jurists in resolving their disputes, unifying their word, addressing their problems, consoling them during adversity, and lending their hands to offer assistance. There was a strong bond between the people and the jurists who played a fatherly role to encompass the believers.

The religious teachings, piety, wisdom, devotion, and drive to reform the affairs of the believers played a pivotal role in bridging the gaps between the jurists and bringing them together to perform their duties. This rich religious culture mitigated their differences and close to unified their position in rallying the Shia together and addressing their problems. Still, the door of *ijtihad* remains open and each jurist has the freedom to state his own position.

---

[11] There are a number of conditions that a jurist must have in order to be qualified for emulation by the Shia. One of the conditions is that he must be "just" at a high degree. Grand Ayatollah Muhammad Saeed Al-Hakeem defines "just" as one who is pious and shields himself from violating any religious obligations and falling into any sin, even minor ones. When a person falls into sin, which should be infrequent, he should rush to seek repentance. –Eds.

[12] Al-Amili, *Wasael Al-Shia*, 18:95.

## Leadership

The *Marjaeya* was able to lead the nation and unify it during the time of the Major Occultation. There is no doubt that divine guidance plays a critical role in overseeing this system, along with the sponsorship of the living Twelfth Imam. The Imam's presence during the time of occultation is like the sun behind the clouds. It cannot be viewed by the eyes, but its presence and benefits are felt everywhere.

## Financial Independence

After the faith was established and settled with the Shia, the Imams succeeding Imam Hussain started to remind the Shia of their right in *Khums*.[13] This right that was nearly forgotten due to the continuous and systematic efforts by the rivals of the Progeny to erase their mentioning.

After gradually reminding the Shia of this right, they urged them to use it as an independent stream of revenue that can support their needs. With the ceaseless persecution of the tyrannical regimes and the exclusion of the Shia from the public treasury, the followers of the Progeny were in dire need for such a financial institution.

The Imams instructed the Shia to depend on each other, collaborate and coordinate with one another, become content, and endure the hardships of life. We previously shed light on the massive voluntary expenditures by the Shia to commemorate the tragedy of Karbala and other important religious occasions. Furthermore, the Shia were generous in

---

[13] *Khums* – literally 'one fifth' – is a type of obligatory almsgiving on certain earnings. –Eds.

funding efforts to propagate the message and to establish the seminaries.

And with the institution of the *Khums*, the seminaries were able to remain financially independent. They were able to manage without relying on government funding. With their independence and self-sustainability, they were respected and revered by the Shia faithful and others. Thus, they were able to maintain the faith by preserving the creed and jurisprudence despite all the odds.

Due to all the previous factors, the Shia presence thrived with a solid establishment, distinct in its creed, jurisprudence, spirituality, and heritage. There was a rich culture and an effective presence for the seminaries and jurists that drove the direction for the believers. This establishment supported four critical matters.

First, they ensured that the faith remains strong and effective. It comported with the *fitrah*[14] and did not have any contradictions or negativities. The message made sense to people. It promoted objective and reasonable inquiry for the truth.

Second, they continued to remind people of the stature of the Progeny, and the Imams continued to command respect from all the Muslims. This instilled a sense of pride for the Shia who held on to the Imams as their role models.

Third, they emphasized belief in Imam Mahdi who guards and sponsors the message and its carriers.

---

[14] *Fitrah* refers to the innate disposition and nature of mankind, which includes, amongst other things, logic, morality, and belief in God's oneness. –Eds.

Fourth, they continued to remind the Shia of the boundless extent of God's bounties. His incredible work and miracles spark life and hope for the continuation of the message.

The result of the success of this establishment is that it became relevant on the ground despite all of the obstacles and the unending conflicts that exist to this day. This presence on the ground did not rely on the support or sponsorship of the governments. Even at times when the Shia establishment did use the government for its advancement, it did not compromise its independence or principles.

## THE CALL OF TRUTH

This was all possible with the tireless efforts of the immaculate progeny of Imam Hussain. They expressed their lack of desire for political authority and dedicated all of their time for their Shia. They continued the mission and capitalized on the grand accomplishments of their predecessors whose wise actions and unmatched sacrifices laid the foundation for the rise and growth of Shia Islam.

All of this work was intended to establish a group that would publically advocate for the truth, practice it, and disseminate it. As God mentions in the Holy Book, *"Among those We have created are a nation who guide by the truth and do justice thereby."*[15]

The Prophet also explains, *"There will be a sect in my nation that will manifest the truth. They will not be harmed even by those who forsake them until God decrees his will…"*[16]

---

[15] They Holy Quran, 7:181.
[16] Al-Nisaburi, *Sahih Muslim*, 6:52-53.

All of this is to raise awareness amongst the people and establish clear proof. With this, anyone who would search for the truth and inquire into its overwhelming evidences can find it.

Islam excelled above all of other faiths because its proof remained and its features did not melt away with the passing of time. Despite unending conflicts and sedition, and despite its many internal and external enemies, the true teachings of the religion of Islam live on. And since Islam is the final message delivered by the Seal of Prophets, its features and characteristics must remain clear, its call always heard, and its proof ever apparent.

That is indeed the reasonable justification and natural explanation for the longevity of the occultation of the Twelfth Imam in a time where there are severe instigations, vicious conflicts, and increased enemies.

In one narration, Imam al-Sadiq described to a close companion the era of the occultation. The Imam described the length of that period and the many deviant paths that will rise during that time. When the companion heard all this, he began to cry. The Imam asked him, "Why do you cry?" The companion answered that he could not hold his tears when he heard about the spread of turmoil and deviance.

Upon hearing this, the Imam pointed to a window through which sunlight entered the room. He asked, "Is this [sun] apparent?" The companion replied in the affirmative. The Imam then declared, "Our matter is more evident than this sun."[17]

---

[17] Al-Kulayni, *Al-Kafi*, 1:338-39.

It appears from these narrations that the message of Islam will be visible and clear during the time of occultation. There will be a faction of righteous individuals that will hold on firmly to the message despite the longevity of the occultation and the spread of distortion, deviance, and degeneracy.

This is evident in the history of the Shia. With the passing of time, Shia Islam and the Shia have continued to thrive, gaining the compassion, respect, and admiration of many. In fact, it has spread far and wide as people accept the words of the Imams and become enlightened by their creed.

The Imams succeeding Imam Hussain were exceptionally successful in advancing the mission of their predecessors. They preserved the trust that they were assigned. They showed people the way and curbed the spread of deviation and immorality. They preserved the faith – in its teachings and its followers. May God reward them and bless us to remain steadfast on their path.

# EPILOGUE

## CLARITY

It should be clear that the Immaculate Imams from the Progeny of the Holy Prophet had made countless sacrifices in their effort to preserve the true faith of Islam. They stood firmly against the tyrants who were willing to fabricate, lie, and distort the religion of the Prophet Muhammad.

Their sacrifices ushered grand victories for the religion of Islam. But these victories were also grand triumphs for all revealed religions and their sacred symbols.

The teachings of the Holy Household drew attention to the fact that these previous revealed religions had been distorted by the oppressors and tyrants of the time. These revealed religions are innocent of the fabricated lies that convey contradictions and fairytales in the form of faith. The divine faiths are innocent of the actions of oppressive tyrants that exploited faith in order to subjugate the masses and strengthen their own positions.

The symbols of these faiths are immaculate leaders chosen by God and hold a special place with Him. They are divine leaders that are innocent of any sin and purified from any evil. They are innocuous of the things that the deviant hands of distortion allege.

The prophets and vicegerents of God exhausted their efforts and sacrificed all they had for the propagation of their divine message. They came to give earnest advice to their nations. They showed their peoples the path of truth, and they were not shaken by any reproach or oppression.

The revelation that the messengers and vicegerents of God deliver must be of a nature that advances society and brings them closer to God the Almighty. This also means that God would not trust his message to anyone but those who are role models in their knowledge, character, and piety. The representatives of God are the most qualified individuals to teach about God's religion and call unto His path. They do this in both speech and action, as the greatest exemplars of God's principles.

To ascribe notions that are in contradiction to this essential foundation would be strictly false and erroneous. It would be an offensive fabrication, even if its source is one who claims to be part of or ascribe to that faith. Therefore, defending the true teachings of Islam is actually an affirmative defense of all other noble faiths. It preserves their sanctity and the sanctity of their leaders.

Thus, if Islam is affected by the hands of corruption and distortion, it is an attack on the integrity of all noble traditions and the preservation of the principles of faith. Society would be stuck between religion deduced to nothing more than mythology and materialistic ideologies that lack in guidance and balance for the seekers of truth. Thus, society would find itself taken by corruption with its values and principles forsaken and forgotten.

Therefore, standing against any distortion in Islam played a great role in preserving a true understanding of the realities relating to God, His messengers and prophets, and His revelation. It made evident the fact that previous religions – and even some portions of Islamic heritage – had been distorted and taken away from the reality of the divine messages.

This is how the tragedy of Karbala played its critical and consequential role in the history of Islam. Simultaneously, it carried the course of God's divinely appointed guardians of faith, as well as impacted human thought overall. Imam Hussain's undying sacrifice reawakened and continues to reawaken the conscience mankind.

## COMMEMORATION

We have made clear in the discussions throughout this book the importance of the commemoration of the tragedy of Karbala, as well as all other occasions of the Progeny. We must visit their holy shrines. We must take care of these sacred places and build them in the best of ways. We must gather to remember their teachings in occasions of happiness and sorrow. We must recite poetry in dedication to them. We must do all this and more for their sake. They taught us, guided us to the righteous path, and gave us everything. They emphasized that we hold tight to these rituals to maintain our strength in creed and identity.

It is important for the reader to pay attention to a number of factors:

*Differences in Rituals*

Keep in mind that people commemorate the tragedies and celebrations of the Progeny in different ways. Each community may express its emotions differently through rituals that are appropriate for its customs and traditions.

Therefore, every community should be enfranchised to practice its rituals in the way it sees best fit to express its emotions, so long as it does not cross the bounds of religious teachings. If a community's expression is restricted, its passion will be reduced and gradually fade away. The community will not be able to carry forward the momentum of commemoration that it has carried for hundreds of years.

History has also taught us that the emotions and the rituals of the commemoration have been kept alive – despite all adversity – by the practice of the great majority of the believers. Because of their sheer numbers, their enemies had trouble removing them. Their commemorations could not be stopped and their emotions could not be smothered. The intellectual foundations of the Shia were protected by the passion they held for the Progeny. That passion was their drive in safeguarding their identity and it could not be extinguished.

This is especially true because of the position that commemorations and celebrations have taken in the heart of the majority of the believers. Because of their love for the Prophet and his Progeny, they cannot be separated from these rituals.

As for the vanguard of the believers – the religious scholars, intellectuals, and the community leaders – they have a special position in support of the call of the truth. Amongst them are those who preserve this call and support it financially and morally. Yet they alone cannot stand against the attacks of the opposition, due to their small number and special qualities.

In fact, enemies may easily undermine their effectiveness. The enemies may physically remove them through assassination. It may stifle their movements by imprisonment, terror tactics, or similar means. They may use bribery and extortion to deviate some.

But the great majority of the believers are the ones who protect this call. They carry its banner and are its sturdy shield. In fact, they are the protectors of the vanguard. By their sheer number and their perseverance, they protect the vanguard, as any attack on the vanguard would not be taken lightly by the majority. They are a force to be reckoned with.

This underscores the importance of allowing the public to partake in the commemorations of these occasions in the way that best expresses their emotions. Rather, they must be encouraged to partake in these rituals so that these occasions take root in their psyche and identity. By this they will be able to fulfill their principled mission effectively and adamantly.

They are valuable assets for the faith, especially in times of crisis. They would stand against the pressures that force the vanguard to sit idly. And while some in the vanguard may even be convinced, for one reason or another, that they must lower morale, we always find that the majority are adamant about these rituals. The rituals took root in their communities, and they are the best fit to protect them. They are less easily pressured and more apt to avoid such pressures. The experiences of Iraq in the wake of the fall of the Baathist regime illustrate this quite well.

What adds to the importance of the participation of the majority is the fact that their vast numbers in expressing their emotions serves to draw attention towards the tragedy. All this makes their rituals a reason for change within their community. Their actions are a call to anyone who does not know and a reminder for the heedless. It encourages individuals who carry this work, allowing them to stand steadfast and continue with conviction.

This is how these rituals leave their imprints on to the fabric of society. It allows society to relate to the tragedy and its principles. It allows people to relive the events of tragedy and draw lessons from the sacrifices made. The tragedy becomes part and parcel of society's psyche, identity, and existence.

And while the vanguard may not be able to participate in these rituals – they may not even be able to give them legitimacy at times – they must, once the opportunity arises, be part of this movement.

They must take part in this so that they can raise the morale of the masses. They must make them feel the importance of their stance when they are partaking in these rituals. They must emphasize the legitimacy of all this and convey their gratitude for what the majority does.

This way, the path is blocked for whoever wants to discourage the public away from their rituals or lessen their meaning.

*Emphatic Rituals*

Emphatic rituals – ones that attract the attention of others – that are usually conducted by the majority of the followers of the Progeny of the Prophet, have a great effect in keeping the tragedy of Karbala alive and allowing it to spread. They are the most expressive of emotions. They show how deeply rooted the tragedy became within the public identity.

These emphatic rituals are also the ones that draw the attention of outside observers. They create curiosity in the mind of anyone who is unfamiliar with the tragedy. Thus, people are drawn towards Imam Hussain because of these emphatic rituals. They seek to learn about the Shia and their rituals. They may even be drawn toward becoming part of the movement and adopting the school of thought of the Progeny of the Holy Prophet.

This sheds some light on a portion of the narration of Muawiya ibn Wahab, relating a supplication of Imam al-Sadiq for the visitors of Imam Hussain.

> *O God, our enemies reproached them. However, it did not deter them from coming out for us to defy those that have defied us. O God have mercy on the faces that were altered by the sun. Have mercy on the cheeks that roll over on the grave of Abu Abdullah Al-Hussain. Have mercy on the eyes that shed tears for us. Have mercy on the hearts that crazed and burned for us. Have mercy on the shout that was made for us. O God I entrust you these bodies and*

*souls until you quench them from the pond on the day of thirst...*[1]

Of course, there must also be a number of calm and tranquil rituals that complement the emphatic ones. This includes the recitation of the saga of Karbala and the gatherings of mourning, supplications to God, and salutations to the Progeny of the Prophet. Each one of the rituals must be employed wisely on a circumstantial basis.

All this is so that attention is drawn to the tragic event and its many deep meanings.

*Evolving Rituals*

Some claim that the rituals of commemoration must evolve in order to suit the time and place of those who wish to commemorate the tragedy. But while we believe that new methods of commemoration must continue to evolve, we also believe that these new methods must complement – not supplant – the traditional rituals of commemoration.

If we look into history, we will see that these traditional rituals had in fact been foreign to the time in which they developed. They were rejected and attacked then, and they will continue to be rejected and attacked. But as they persevere, they continue to achieve their intended goal. And as their foreign nature did not stop them in times of old, it will not stop them in the present or in the future.

The world is full of groups – religious, ethnic, or otherwise – that have their own cultures, traditions, and rituals. The fact that they may take part in some rituals that are specific

---

[1] Al-Qummi, *Kamil Al-Ziyarat*, 228-229.

to their group does not justify the rejection and attacks of others, even if their rituals were seen as foreign in the environment directly surrounding them.

There is no reason to fear or feel weak simply because these rituals are foreign to some. So long as they fulfill their required role of expressing the emotions of mourning, they should not be replaced with anything that may be less expressive or mournful.

We should not give undue weight to pleasing others or to evading their attacks and vilification. This would only lead to the imagining of negative consequences and implications that do not in fact exist.

And since the intent behind such attacks and vilification is to stop the Shia from continuing with their rituals, we should not allow these attempts the opportunity of success by backing down from our legitimate right to express our passion. If we remain resolute, these attacks will begin to dwindle and die down. The opponents of these rituals will realize that the mourning of Imam Hussain will remain a constant reality and a perseverant remembrance of the principles of faith.

*Differing Opinions*

At times, differing opinions may arise with respect to the rituals of mourning. Some of it may be based on the scholarly deduction of jurists. It may be due to a difference in the weighing of countervailing evidence that may change the religious ruling based on some secondary principles.

At that point, both sides of the disagreement must remain civil in representing their point of view. They may attempt to convince one another using kind words and sound reason, as our faith always teaches us. It should not be escalated to hostile confrontation and vilification of the other side. This would only lead to disunity and schisms amongst the followers of the school of thought of the Progeny.

Much effort is wasted on such arguments when these efforts are sorely needed for strengthening the school of thought and its followers. So long as Islam remains deprived of an Immaculate guide who can directly influence the conversation, differences will remain. And in this circumstance, no party can force its opinion onto others.

*Rituals as a Stance Against Oppression*

There are some who limit the rituals of commemoration to being a stance against oppression and injustice. Thus, they become mere traditions and insignificant practices when they are not being performed in direct opposition to a tyrant.

This is clearly erroneous. For one, these acts have been unequivocally endorsed by the Immaculate Imams without limitation to being a stance against oppression and injustice. And when the Shia initiated these practices – at the behest of their divinely chosen leaders – they did not pursue them as a direct confrontation to the tyrants of the time. In fact, the rituals were initiated on an individual basis and in secrecy so as to avoid the ire of the ruling authorities. Thus, the only purpose behind them was the word and emphasis of the Progeny.

As we discussed, these commemorations were a source of strength for the Shia. When successive tyrannical authorities realized this strength, they began to persecute anyone who commemorated the tragedies of the Progeny. And as persecution persisted, the Shia persevered. Thus, the confrontation with these tyrants was incidental to – and not a feature, cause, or condition of – these commemorations.

*Etiquettes of Commemoration*

The believers who wish to commemorate the tragedy of Karbala must at all times be cognizant of the etiquettes and purpose of these commemorations.

They must preserve their sacred nature and not take them out of the bounds of permissibility, as drawn by the teachings of the faith. Those who commemorate these tragedies must always be exemplars in ethics and piety.

These commemorations are done in the service of the Progeny of our Prophet. In these events, all personal conflicts must be forgotten – or at least ignored. We must focus on our shared values and purpose so that we can best serve our respective communities.

The organizers of these events must exert their energies and efforts in creating an atmosphere of mourning and sorrow. The commemoration of the tragedies of the Progeny must draw tears from the audience. Those who exert their creative energy and efforts to give something new to the crowd must always keep this in mind. The purpose behind these commemorations is not to express creativity and skills, but to express the deep sorrow that manifested from the tragedy.

Finally, the commemorations of the tragedies of the Progeny should not be a stage for flexing. They should not be used as proving grounds for personal skills or popularity. All this is beneath the sacred nature of these events.

These are spiritual events that must be marked with the remembrance of God and His divinely chosen vicegerents. They are events that must be kept free of all inappropriate elements and behaviors. So just as they must be purged of personal competition and rivalries, they must also be purified of any impermissibility – such as music and extravagance.

And just as this is true for occasions of commemoration, it is also true for the special occasions that are marked with celebrations and festivities. These are occasions on which God's emissaries are remembered and honored. They must befit their pious and ethical character.

As we continue in our commemorations and celebrations, we must always be mindful of God and thankful for the blessing of guidance. We must show gratitude for His guidance which allowed us to take these individuals as role models.

So let those who administer these commemorations and celebrations be mindful of the fact that the Immaculate leaders of this nation – especially the Twelfth Holy Imam – are ever present in these gatherings. We must ensure that these gatherings are appropriate and worthy of their presence.

More importantly, let the organizers of these events be mindful that God, the Omniscient, is ever aware of their deeds and their intentions. They must keep Him at the forefront of their minds and serve in a way that pleases Him and is within the boundaries of His faith.

## Importance of Individual Efforts

It should be obvious that the reason for commemorating and celebrating these occasions is love and devotion to the Progeny of our Prophet. It is narrated that Imam Ali said,

> God, the Exalted and Glorified, looked over the Earth and selected us. He selected for us followers that support us. They are pleased for our happiness, and mourn for our sorrows. They expend their wealth and their being for us. They are of us and to us.[2]

Thus, each believer is driven by devotion to express the passion of love and admiration. The lack of public gatherings, organizational capacities, and personal skills are not limits for these individuals. Their expression springs from their hearts and is not stymied by lack of resources and capacities. Every effort, no matter how small, will be accepted – God willing.

Masma', a companion of Imam al-Sadiq, narrates that the Imam once asked him, "Oh Masma', you are of the people of Iraq. Do you not reach the grave of Hussain?" Masma' replied, "No. I am a man well known amongst the people of Basra. We have amongst us men who follow the whims of this caliph. Our enemies are many, from the people of the tribes, fanatic opponents, and others. I do not trust them, lest they confer [the reality of] my [beliefs] to the [governors], who would assail me."

---

[2] Al-Sadouq, *Al-Khisal*, 635.

Imam al-Sadiq asked him, "Do you not remember what was done to [Hussain]?"

"Yes," Masma' replied.

"Do you anguish [at the thought]?" Imam al-Sadiq continued.

"Yes, by God," Masma' cried. "I weep for it until my family can see it in me. I refrain from eating until it becomes apparent in my face."

The Imam would then assure him,

> *May God have mercy on your tear. You will be counted amongst those who anguish for us. They are pleased for our happiness, and mourn for our sorrows. They are fearful for our insecurity, and are at peace when we are secure.*
>
> *Surely, you will see at the moment of your passing the presence of my forefathers, and how they will request of the Angel of Death [to take care of] you. What they will give you of glad tidings is much greater. The Angel of Death will be more compassionate and merciful with you than a mother caring for her child.*[3]

This is one of the important factors behind the resilience of the school of thought of the Progeny. Their devotees are not limited by lack of numbers or capabilities. They carry their tragedies in their hearts no matter where they are. And once the circumstances arise to undertake the rituals of mourning, they are always ready to express their grief.

---

[3] Al-Qummi, *Kamil Al-Ziyarat*, 203-04.

## Divine Rewards

Many narrations emphasize the importance of bringing life to the rituals of the Progeny, especially commemoration of the tragedy of Karbala and visitation of the shrine of Imam Hussain. They contain promises of great rewards, forgiveness of sins, guarantees of paradise, and more. If anything, this indicates the great importance placed on the commemoration and celebration of the life and sacrifices of the Progeny – an importance that suits the great triumphs that they achieved in preserving and strengthening the faith.

# REFERENCED WORKS

## SCRIPTURE

The Holy Quran

The Bible, Kings James Version

## OTHER SOURCES

Al-Aalusi, Shihad Al-Deen. *Rooh Al-Ma'ani.*

Al-Andalusi, Ahmad ibn Muhammad. *Al-'Iqd Al-Fareed.* Beirut: Daar Al-Kitab Al-Arabi, 1405 AH.

Al-Asfahani, Abu Al-Faraj. *Al-Aghani.* Beirut: Daar Al-Kutub.

Al-Asfahani, Abu Al-Faraj. *Maqatil Al-Talibiyyin.* Najaf: Al-Maktaba Al-Haydariya, 1965 CE.

Al-Asqalani, ibn Hajar. *Al-Isaba fi Ma'rifat Al-Sahaba.* Beirut: Daar Al-Kutub Al-Ilmiyya, 1995 CE.

Al-Bahrani, Abdullah ibn Noorullah. *Awalim Al-'Uloom.* Qum: Ameer, 1407 AH.

Al-Balathiri, Ahmad ibn Yahya ibn Jabir. *Ansaab Al-Ashraaf.* Beirut: Daar Al-Fikr, 1996 CE.

Al-Bayhaqi, Ibrahim ibn Muhammad. *Al-Mahasin wa Al-Masawi.* Egypt: Al-Sa'ada, 1906 CE.

Al-Bukhari, Muhammad ibn Ismail. *Sahih Al-Bukhari*. Beirut: Daar Al-Fikr, 1401 AH.

Al-Darimi, Abdullah ibn Abdulrahman. *Sunan Al-Darimi*. Damascus: Al-I'tidal, 1349 AH.

Al-Daynouri, Abdullah ibn Muslim. *Al-Imama wa Al-Siyasa*. Beirut: Daar Al-Kutub Al-Ilmiyya, 1997 CE.

Al-Fayrouzabadi, Muhammad ibn Yaqoub. *Sifr Al-Sa'ada*. Egypt: Daar Al Usoor, 1332 AH.

Al-Haythami, Imam Ali ibn Abubakr. *Majma' Al-Zawaed wa Manba' Al-Fawaid*. Beirut: Daar Al-Kutub Al-Ilmiyya, 1988 CE.

Al-Hindi, Imam Ali Al-Muttaqi. *Kanz Al-Ummal fi Sunan Al-Aqwal wa Al-Af'aal*. Beirut: Mu'assasat Al-Risala, 1989 CE.

Al-Khawarizmi, Al-Muwaffaq ibn Ahmad. *Al-Manaqib*. Qum: Mu'assasat Al-Nashr Al-Islami, 1411 AH.

Al-Kufi, Ahmad ibn A'tham. *Al-Futuh*. Beirut: Daar Al-Kutub Al-Ilmiyya, 1986 CE.

Al-Kulayni, Muhammad ibn Yaqoub. *Al-Kafi*. Tehran: Daar Al-Kutub Al-Islamiyya, 1388 AH.

Al-Mutazili, ibn Abu Al-Hadeed. *Sharh Nahj Al-Balagha*. Daar Ihya Al-Kutub Al-Arabiyya, 1959 CE.

Al-Najafi, Muhammad Hassan. *Jawahir Al-Kalaam fi Sharh Sharae' Al-Islam*. Tehran: Khorsheed, 1365 SH.

Al-Nisaburi, Muhammad ibn Abdullah. *Al-Mustadrak*. Cairo: Daar al-Taaseel.

Al-Nisaburi, Muslim ibn Al-Hajjaj. *Sahih Muslim*. Beirut: Daar Al-Fikr.

Al-Qummi, Jafar ibn Muhammad ibn Qawlaweih. *Kamil Al-Ziyarat*. Qum: Mu'assasat Al-Nashr Al-Islami, 1417 AH.

Al-Qunduzi, Suleiman ibn Ibrahim. *Yanabee' Al-Mawadda li Thawi Al-Qurba*. Daar Al-Uswa, 1416 AH.

Al-Qurtubi, ibn Abdulbar Al-Nimri. *Al-Isti'ab fi Ma'rifat Al-Ashaab*. Beirut: Daar Al-Jeel, 1412 AH.

Al-Qurtubi, Yousef ibn Abdullah. *Jami' Bayan Al-Ilm wa Fadlih.* Beirut: Daar Al-Kutub Al-Ilmiyya, 1398 AH.

Al-Radi, Muhammad ibn Al-Hussain. *Nahj Al-Balagha.* Beirut: Daar Al-Ma'rifa, 1412 AH.

Al-Sadouq, Muhammad ibn Ali. *Kamal Al-Deen wa Tamam Al-Ni'ma.* Qum: Mu'assasat Al-Nashr Al-Islami, 1405 AH.

Al-Sadouq, Muhammad ibn Ali. *Al-Khisal.* Qum: Jama'at Al-Mudarrisseen, 1403 AH.

Al-San'ani, Abdulrazzaq ibn Humam. *Al-Musannaf.* Almajlis Al-Ilmi.

Al-Shaybani, Ahmad ibn Hanbal. *Musnad Ahmad ibn Hanbal.* Beirut: Daar Saadir.

Al-Siyouti, Jalal Al-Deen. *Al-Durr Al-Manthoor fi Al-Tafseer bi Al-Ma'thoor.* Beirut: Daar Al-Fikr

Al-Tabarani, Suleiman ibn Ahmad. *Al-Mu'jam Al-Kabir.* Beirut: Daar Ihya' Al-Turath Al-Arabi.

Al-Tabari, Muhammad ibn Jareer ibn Rustum. *Dalael Al-Imama.* Qum: Mu'assasat Al-Bi'tha, 1413 AH.

Al-Tabari, Muhammad ibn Jareer ibn Yazid. *Tareekh Al-Umam wa Al-Mulk (Tareekh Al-Tabari).* Beirut: Mu'assasat Al-A'lami, 1983 CE.

Al-Tabrasi, Ahmad ibn Ali. *Al-Ihtijaj.* Najaf: Daar Al-Nu'man.

Al-Dhahabi, Muhammad ibn Ahamd. *Tathkirat Al-Hoffadh.* Beirut: Daar Ihya' Al-Turath Al-Arabi.

Al-Dhahabi, Muhammad ibn Ahmad. *Siyar A'lam Al-Nubala.* Beirut: Mu'assasat Al-Risala, 1413 AH.

Al-Tousi, Muhammad ibn Al-Hassan. *Misbah Al-Mutahajjid.* Beirut: Mu'assasat Fiqh Al-Shia, 1991 CE.

Al-Yaqoubi, Ahmad ibn Abu Yaqoub ibn Jafar Al-Abbasi. *Tareekh Al-Yaqoubi.* Beirut: Daar Saadir.

Arastu, Rizwan. *God's Emissaries.* Dearborn: Imam Mahdi Association of Marjaeya, 2014 CE.

Ibn Abu Jurada, Omar ibn Ahmad. *Bughyat Al-Talab fi Tareekh Halab.* Beirut: Daar Al-Fikr.

Ibn Abu Shayba, Abdullah ibn Muhammad. *Al-Musannaf.* Beirut: Daar Al-Fikr, 1989 CE.

Ibn Al-Atheer, Imam Ali ibn Abu Al-Karam. *Usud Al-Ghaba fi Ma'rifat Al-Sahaba.* Beirut: Daar Al-Kitab Al-Arabi.

Ibn Al-Atheer, Muhammad ibn Muhammad. *Al-Kamil fi Al-Tareekh.* Beirut: Daar Saadir, 1965 CE.

Ibn Asakir, Imam Ali ibn Al-Hassan. *Tareekh Dimashq.* Beirut: Daar Al-Fikr, 1995 CE.

Ibn Katheer, Ismail ibn Omar. *Al-Bidaya wa Al-Nihaya.* Beirut: Daar Ihya Al-Turath Al-Arabi, 1988 CE.

Ibn Shahrashoob, Muhammad ibn Ali. *Manaqib Aal Abu Talib.* Najaf: Al-Matba'a Al-Haydariyya, 1376 AH.

Ibn Tawuus, Imam Ali ibn Musa. *Al-Luhuf fi Qatla Al-Tufoof.* Qum: Anwar Al-Huda, 1417 AH.

Ibn Tayfour, Abu Al-Fadl ibn Abu Tahir. *Balaghat Al-Nisa.* Qum: Maktabat Basirati.

Sibt ibn Al-Jawzi, Yousef ibn Farghali. *Tathkirat Al-Khawas.* Najaf: Al-Maktaba Al-Haydariyya, 1964 CE.

www.ingramcontent.com/pod-product-compliance
Lightning Source LLC
Chambersburg PA
CBHW021223090426
42740CB00006B/358